SIMPLIFY
YOUR LIFE
WITH KIDS

SIMPLIFY YOUR LIFE WITH KIDS

100 Ways to Make Family Life Easier and More Fun

ELAINE ST. JAMES

with Vera Cole

Andrews McMeel Publishing

Kansas City

Library of Congress Cataloging-in-Publication Data

St. James, Elaine.
Simplify your life with kids : 100 ways to make family life easier and more fun / Elaine St. James with Vera Cole.
p.   cm.
ISBN 0–8362–3595–9 (hd)
1. Family—United States.   2. Family—Time management—United States.
3. Parenting—United States.   4. Simplicity.   I. Cole, Vera.   II. Title.
HQ536.S7175   1997
646.7′8—dc21
97–15340
CIP

98 99 00 01 RDC 10 9 8 7

ATTENTION: SCHOOLS AND BUSINESSES

Andrews McMeel books are available at quantity discounts with bulk purchase for educational, business, or sales promotional use. For information, please write to: Special Sales Department, Andrews McMeel Publishing, 4520 Main Street, Kansas City, Missouri 64111.

ALSO BY ELAINE ST. JAMES

Simplify Your Life

Inner Simplicity

Living the Simple Life

To my parents
A. J. and Dorothy Kennedy

To my husband
Wolcott Gibbs, Jr.

To our kids
Bill, Michelle, Eric, and Lisa;

To "my" kids
Karin, Jim, Ellen, Dave, Joanie, and Joe;
Mark, Kathie, and Bill;
Marisa, Tiffany, Kim, and Amie

To their kids
Jessie and Megan;
Jennifer, Seth, Corey, and Chad;
Adrienne, Natalie, and Eric;
Benjamin, Elizabeth, and Sam;
Debbie and Benjamin

To Peter, Sasha, and Andrew

And to all the parents and children of Orcas Island

In loving memory of Sue Pettengill
1942–1997

Contents

"Why didn't somebody tell me it would be this hard?" xvii

Three: THE STUFF

Four: THE PLUGGED-IN FAMILY

Five: THE INDEPENDENT CHILD

Contents

Six: SIMPLE PARENTING PRACTICES

Seven: SIMPLE DISCIPLINE STRATEGIES

Eight: CONFLICT

Contents

Nine: *FAMILY ISSUES*

Ten: *SIMPLE HOLIDAYS AND CELEBRATIONS*

Eleven: *AT SCHOOL*

Fifteen: THE MOST IMPORTANT THING

"Why didn't somebody tell me it would be this hard?"

ANY WEEKDAY, 5:30 P.M. You've just arrived home after a grueling day at work. You rescued your two-year-old from the baby-sitter and managed to pick up your seven-year-old from her dance class. You were supposed to meet your ten-year-old after his Little League practice fifteen minutes ago, but you completely lost track of time.

When the phone rings you run to answer it, hoping your son has found a ride home, but it's your daughter's teacher—there's a problem at school. You search frantically for a pencil so you can jot down some notes, but all you can find is a broken crayon.

You hear the beep from call waiting, put the teacher on hold, and realize you've picked up a call from someone soliciting subscriptions for the local paper.

You get rid of that call and your toddler begins to whine. You know he's hungry and you should be starting dinner, but you can't do anything until you get off the phone, fetch your ten-year-old, and clean up the mess from the breakfast dishes.

As you quietly try to soothe your child, call waiting beeps again. It's the Brownie troop leader, asking when she can come by to pick up the two dozen cookies you promised for the bake sale. Suddenly, your seven-year-old decides now is a good time to show you her drawing and wants to know if you like it. Your son starts crying hysterically—he's tired of waiting and wants something to eat right now.

You're still juggling two phone calls and two children when your spouse arrives home wanting attention, dinner, and some peace and quiet.

You greet your husband—and patiently explain why he has to go back out to pick up your ten-year-old. You finish your calls, and miraculously get dinner on the table.

But when you finally sit down to eat, it's chaos—the children don't like the meal you prepared, conversation with your spouse is next to impossible, and the phone doesn't stop ringing.

By the time dinner is over you're completely frazzled, everyone's upset, and you're dreading bath time, bedtime, and the challenge of tearing your kids away from the TV.

You manage to get everyone tucked in, and you finally crawl into bed too tired to sleep. You murmur a silent prayer that your two-year-old doesn't wake up again at three A.M. with a nightmare. And you wonder if there'll ever come a day when you don't feel completely overwhelmed and exhausted.

You love your kids. You wouldn't trade them for anything in the world. But you think *there's got to be an easier way.*

. . .

There is an easier way. There are many easier ways. That's what this book is all about. It outlines over one hundred things you can do to eliminate most of the complications that cause scenarios like this to be played out in the lives of millions of families every day.

One of the biggest complaints parents have is that there aren't enough hours in the day to do the things they feel they have to do. But they want more than time. They want their lives to be free of the pressures that make it difficult, if not impossible, to enjoy that time.

I know what it's like to live a hectic life. Several years ago in a quiet moment I discovered that my time-management system weighed close to six pounds—and for all practical purposes it was chained to my wrist. I took some time off to contemplate how absurd it was for me to have been living at a pace that made this seem perfectly natural. Then my husband, Gibbs, and I made the decision to change our lifestyle so we could live more simply. I wrote a little book about our experiences in this venture, *Simplify Your Life: 100 Ways to Slow Down and Enjoy the Things That Really Matter.*

I soon began getting letters from readers. Many were parents who shared their own experiences in simplifying. But there were many other parents who said things like, "That's fine, but how can you possibly simplify your life if you've got kids?"

My step-sons were grown and on their own when Gibbs and I decided to simplify, so we hadn't gone through the process with them in tow. But I knew that, with or without kids, the basic principles of simplifying were the same: We have to deal with the daily routines, our workloads, our buying habits, and the stuff we often mindlessly accumulate. And we have to learn to say no to many of the work, social, and civic requests that rob us of the time we want for ourselves and our families.

But simplifying with kids also means dealing with a multitude of other issues. Chronic fatigue, a scarcity of time and money, and the never-ending stream of laundry are only the beginning. There are also the constant worries: Are your kids happy? Are they growing as they should? Do they have nice friends, polite manners, good grades? Is the baby-sitter treating them well? Are you doing everything right? And then there are the routine problems that range from runny noses, tantrums, and separation anxiety to spilled milk, kids' birthday parties, and deciding who gets to sit in the front seat of the car.

So when it came time to write this book, I called on my good friend, Vera Cole. As parents of three children—Peter, seventeen, Sasha, fourteen, and Andrew, six—Vera and her husband, Tim, know what it's like to have a complicated life. Over the past twenty years I've watched their lives go from the first years of married bliss to the increasing complications of trying to maintain active careers—he as a writer and publisher; she as a writing, teaching, working-from-home mom—while raising a growing family. Like many couples, they struggled with the seemingly endless demands of marriage, jobs, kids, debt, and everyone else's expectations while raising their first two children. But by the time they were ready to have their third child, they were determined to do it differently: they made the commitment to start living saner, simpler lives.

Simplify Your Life with Kids combines my own experiences in simplifying with the wisdom Vera acquired from her process of simplifying with her kids. And it includes many of the ideas readers, friends, relatives, and other families have graciously shared with me.

This is a practical, hands-on guide. My goal is to help you free up time to spend with your kids, doing the things you really want to do. I've started with some of the day-to-day problems that revolve around the morning routine, the household chores, and the accumulation of stuff—many of which are relatively easy to simplify. If you can free up time in these areas, it will make it easier for you to go on to the sometimes more challenging issues of independence, conflict, discipline, and teaching your kids about the facts of life that all parents face at one time or another.

Raising happy, healthy, well-adjusted children is one of our greatest challenges. Kids require incredible amounts of our love, understanding, patience, praise, nurturance, guidance, respect, and thought. And these things all take time. If you can simplify even one or two areas of your life, it will vastly improve the quality and increase the quantity of the time you have to spend with your kids. And your family life will be so much easier and a lot more fun. As it should be.

One
THE DAILY ROUTINE

1.

Eliminate Morning Madness

ONE EASY FIRST STEP you can take to simplify your life with kids is to create an unhurried morning routine.

If you're used to a hectic schedule, you may think tranquil mornings are an impossibility. But I assure you that if you make just few changes in your schedule, it will make a big difference in your entire day.

Some ways to alleviate morning madness include:

1. Set reasonable bedtimes for yourself as well as for the kids so no one's tired and cranky in the morning. Then get up so you have plenty of time to get ready for the day without having to rush. Allow at least an hour to get everyone dressed and fed and to take care of last-minute emergencies.

   Experiment to see how much time your family actually requires, and be willing to change your wake-up times as your schedules change or according to your needs. One child may have an earlier school bus departure, or another may simply move at a slower pace in the morning.

2. Divide the responsibility for younger kids between the parents and the older children. In Vera's family, each member cues the next, so that everyone makes it out of the house on time.

   Her husband, Tim, sets his radio alarm to chime at six A.M. He then listens for Peter to begin—and end—his shower before taking his own shower. Tim wakes up Sasha on the way in. When he finishes his shower, he checks to make sure Sasha is getting dressed for school.

   Meanwhile, Vera has gotten ready for her day, keeping Andrew on schedule.

   After breakfast, Peter catches his seven o'clock bus. At seven-thirty Tim takes Sasha to her bus and goes off to work. Then Vera makes sure Andrew meets his eight o'clock bus.

3. Teach your kids to set out their clothes the night before so you can avoid last-minute scrounging for clean socks, lost shoes, or a favorite shirt. When my friend Cyndy's daughter was seven years old she started making a game out of carefully arranging her clothes for the next day on the floor by her bed. She delighted in making it look as though a small child had lain on the floor, then disappeared, leaving only her clothes behind.

4. Although it may take longer in the beginning, encourage self-sufficiency and cooperation. By ages six or seven, most kids are capable of dressing themselves and preparing their own cereal

in the morning. Have kids do as much as they can on their own, and get older siblings to help their younger brothers and sisters.

5. Kids who take their lunch to school can make it the night before and refrigerate it. Or if the school cafeteria food is acceptable to you and your kids, consider having your children buy school lunches. It's more expensive, but it eliminates last-minute grocery shopping, dirty lunch boxes, and moldy thermoses that have to be cleaned out—or retrieved when they get left on the school bus.

6. Insist that all homework be completed the night before so your child isn't weeping over unfinished assignments or rushing to finish the science project due that day.

   And be sure to designate a convenient place, perhaps on their own desks or a table near the door, where the kids can leave their schoolbags when they've finished their homework. This avoids that last-minute search for misplaced papers when they're trying to catch the bus the next morning.

7. Establish a policy for morning phone use (#33), then stick with it. Allow no outgoing calls except for emergencies, such as a sick child who won't be meeting the car pool. Resist the temptation to answer the phone in the morning. Instead, use the answering machine to screen incoming calls. Ask relatives, friends, and coworkers not to phone you before nine A.M. unless it's urgent.

8. Set the breakfast table the night before—after the dinner dishes are cleaned. This can be included in the chores list (#10) and

makes it easier for you to attend to more important matters, such as taking time at breakfast to talk about the upcoming events of each child's day. You'll have the opportunity to provide support and encouragement for whatever challenges they might be facing—such as a test or a class presentation.

9. Keep TVs, radios, CD players, and Walkmans turned off in the morning. These are major distractions that only add to morning chaos.

10. Do whatever you have to do to meet the car pool or the school bus on time. It will complicate your day to have to make an extra car trip in the morning. It's much easier to leave five minutes early and have time for a quiet chat with your child than to wonder whether you've missed the bus, and then have to go chasing off to school in the car.

11. Put washing the breakfast dishes on your chores list, and make sure they're done before you leave the house. It's so depressing to come home to a sink full of dirty dishes.

12. If you have a recurring complication in your morning routine, take some time to think it through. Come up with practical solutions for your own circumstances that will eliminate morning madness. Do what you need to do so that you have a few moments every morning to truly delight in the joy and the wonder and the fun that kids can bring to your life when you give them your time and attention.

2.

Make Saying Good-bye Easier

AT SOME POINT each day you'll have to say good-bye to your kids. Getting left behind can be especially traumatic for toddlers and preschoolers, but there are things you can do to make it simpler.

For some kids it's easier to say good-bye to Dad, whom they've seen go off to work every day, than it is to leave Mom, who's been their primary caretaker for the first months or years of their lives. So one way to make those first good-byes simpler is to let the parent the child has spent the most time with off the hook, and to have the other parent or another adult take the child to the baby-sitter or to school for a week or so. Sometimes this alone will do the trick.

Plan to spend an extra five or ten minutes with your child when you drop her off at child care or the baby-sitter. Do the same when you pick her up at the end of the day, at least until she gets comfortable with the routine. This eases the transition for very young children who are going from you to the child-care provider and back to you again.

Whatever you do, don't let your kids think they have a choice in the matter of your departure. If they sense that you're hesitating or feeling guilty, they'll scream louder and put up more of a fight. You'll feel worse, and you'll still have to leave. When it's time for you to go, it's better simply to say good-bye and make your exit.

This is true whether you're leaving the kids at child care, with a teacher at school, or at home with a sitter. You'll have to harden your heart momentarily to the bloodcurdling screams, the tear-streaked cheeks, and the imploring outstretched arms begging you not to leave. But your child will invariably stop crying the minute you leave.

Many parents won't leave their kids with a baby-sitter because of this separation anxiety—they can't stand the guilt when their child cries, "Daddy, don't go!" But this only makes leaving more difficult. In the meantime your child has learned to manipulate you, and you're exhausted because you've never had a break. Children need to learn to trust other adults, and these ordinary departures are a safe way to start.

Children can start or stop feeling separation anxiety at any age, though it's most common between nine months and four years of age.

Acute separation anxiety should be regarded as a warning sign that the child may not be ready to be left, or that the caretaker may not be nurturing or attentive. In the worse case, the caretaker may be abusive. Further investigation is warranted if your child continues to cry long after you've gone, or if you notice other behavioral changes when she's back home.

Never, ever sneak out. Tell your children what you're doing, where you're going, and when you'll be back. Then say good-bye and leave. If you sneak out, the next time you try to leave the uproar will be horrific.

A regular routine makes separating easier. Children feel more confident when they know what's going to happen next. Try not to deviate from the schedule in the beginning so your child will know when you're leaving, when you'll be back, and that she'll be okay in the meantime.

Coming home can sometimes be as tricky as leaving. Your kids want your complete attention; they'll pull at you, sit on you, talk, insist, and pester you until they get it. If they don't get it, the situation escalates, and they'll scream and misbehave, even if it means they'll get scolded—which they sometimes prefer to getting no attention at all.

The simplest strategy when coming home is to focus on your kids the minute you walk in the door, before you do anything else. Ask about their day, read to them, play with blocks, draw with them, get them involved in an activity they enjoy. Once you've shown them you love them and are interested in them, it'll be easier for you to go on to whatever you need to do.

In chapter 5 I've outlined other separation tactics that will help make your kids even more independent (#29).

3.

Have Family Meals Together

STUDIES SHOW that the most common factor in happy families is that they have their meals together. Do what you can to arrange your evening meal so you can all sit down to dinner as a family, especially when your kids are young. Once your kids become teenagers, their schedules will often conflict with dinnertime. Then you can put aside one night—Sunday evenings, for example—when the family dinner takes priority over any other activities.

Make meals a pleasant experience everyone looks forward to. Prepare the same meal for everybody, but make sure it includes at least one thing each child likes. If a child decides he doesn't like what's being served, he can get a bowl of cereal or make himself a sandwich.

Avoid getting into the habit of making a separate meal for a picky child. Doing so doubles your preparation and cleanup time and encourages finicky behavior.

If some family members will be eating later, prepare a meal that's easy to reheat. Keep your pantry well stocked with staples such as canned tomatoes, olives, olive oil, spices, tuna, pasta, and rice so someone can always put a quick meal together without having to run to the store. Or prepare large quantities of casseroles or soups and freeze them in serving portions so they can be reheated and served.

Start when your kids are young having them help with meal preparation as part of their regular chores—but don't make it *feel* like a chore to them. Rather, approach it as a natural part of what you do together as a family. When they contribute in this way it'll give you more time with one another, it'll make them more independent (#28), and it eventually relieves you from having to do it all (#13).

When you're all sitting down to dinner, direct the conversation to the day's activities—who did what, where, why, and with whom. Make sure everyone gets a turn to speak. Allow no interruptions when someone is talking. Keep the discussion going by asking specific questions, but don't pry or judge.

Teach the table manners that are important to you by your example and by quiet instruction rather than by reprimanding. "Honey, when is the spring concert? Remember to chew with your mouth closed" focuses attention on the conversation rather than on the behavior.

As you did with the morning meal, establish a policy for handling phone calls, then make sure everyone abides by it.

At the end of the meal, check the chores list to see who clears and who washes, and make sure there's no bickering over who does what. Help your children with their tasks when they're young and you'll make doing chores faster and more fun for them and also extend the time you have together as a family.

As they get older and become more competent in the kitchen, you can leave the cleanup entirely to the kids and begin your own evening activities.

4.

Establish a Regular Bath Routine

THINK OF BATH TIME as the first step toward settling your child down for the evening. The simplest way to make bath time easy for your kids and for you is to make it predictable.

Arrange your evening schedule so that your kids know bath time comes right before (or right after) dinner, and that they get to stay in the bath for a certain amount of time. If you change bath times from night to night, or let your kids stay in the tub for an hour one night and zip them in and out again another night, bathing will be an unsettling rather than a soothing experience.

Don't feel you have to bathe your children every night. They can have a bath every other night if it suits your schedule better.

Having a small supply of interesting toys helps make bath time fun. Rubber animals, boats, scuba divers, or rubber duckies are some possibilities to consider. Andrew didn't seriously get into taking baths until he got a snorkeling mask. (Store bath toys in a net bag with a small cord at the top, which you can hang over the faucet while they drip-dry.)

And you always have your ace in the hole—bubbles. Kids love

making hairdos with bubbles. They practice shaving with them, plaster the wall with them, and play hide-and-seek with their toys with them. Bubbles will keep a child happy for about twenty minutes. Then, just as the last of the bubbles disappear, you can whisk her out of the tub.

Never leave a child in the bath unsupervised. A small child can drown in as little as an inch of water.

Be sure the bathroom is child-friendly: a nonslip rubber pad at the bottom of the tub for safety; a sturdy step stool at the sink; and towels, toothbrushes, hairbrushes, soap, and cups that kids can reach.

Be sure your kids get in the habit of brushing their teeth as part of both their morning and their evening routines. Until they're about five or six, kids are too young to do a thorough job of brushing their teeth on their own, and they'll need your help. Play a simple game of cleaning imaginary animals away from their teeth. Chase around a wily giraffe, go after that silly aardvark, or track down those ol' sugar bugs.

My friend Jane makes this a fun event that she and her four-year-old, Zach, both look forward to. He says, "Okay, Mommy, you hold me and we'll both brush!"

As they get older you can show your kids the proper way to brush by brushing your own teeth. Kids love to imitate their parents. If they see you brushing away, they'll follow your example, especially if you make it seem like fun.

If your child decides she doesn't want to brush, try logical consequences (#41). If she doesn't brush, she doesn't get a bedtime story. Or she doesn't get dessert. ("Sorry, honey, the dentist said no sweets if you don't brush.")

Keep toothbrushes downstairs, too, if possible, so kids can easily brush after meals.

Make bathing a ritual both you and your kids look forward to. Approach these few precious moments of closeness and playfulness as one of the highlights of your day with your kids, and enjoy bath times thoroughly while they last.

5.

Establish a Simple Bedtime Routine

GOING TO BED can be delightful and inviting to a tired child, especially if you establish a simple routine your child can look forward to. This can include a bath, a short playtime, a bedtime story, a snuggle, then lights out.

Be sure to set a reasonable bedtime, and avoid roughhousing, sibling interference, unsettling television programs, or family squabbles. These will sabotage your efforts to get your child to sleep easily.

It's important to keep bedtime consistent. Decide what time you want your child to go to bed and at what time lights should be out, and then stay firm. Except for special occasions, try not to deviate from the schedule. Children need their sleep, and they benefit from a regular routine. And it's important for you to have some quiet time in the evening to recoup your energies. That's easier to do once the kids are tucked in.

A child's bedtime often has to fit with a parent's schedule. Andrew has a nine o'clock bedtime, with lights out at nine-thirty. This may be late for some families, but Tim doesn't get home until seven, and he and Vera want to make sure he has time with Andrew every evening.

Sasha goes to bed at nine-thirty and turns out the lights at ten. Children over ten are capable of putting themselves to bed. All they need is a cue from you, and a good-night hug and kiss before lights-out. On weekends, bedtimes can be extended by half an hour or so.

Once kids hit their middle teens you'll want to be more flexible, depending on their needs, their schedule, and their level of maturity. Peter is usually in bed before his younger siblings, unless he's working on a time-consuming homework project. But there are many teens who would stay up half the night—spending most of it on the phone—if their parents allowed them to. Set a phone curfew, and don't allow your kids to accept calls after that time.

Set bedtimes that are realistic. If you find you're frantically rushing through the evening just to meet the bedtime you've set, move it back by fifteen minutes.

After you've had your quiet time together with snuggles, hugs, kisses, and story time, say your good nights, turn out the lights, and quietly leave the room.

If your child starts to scream bloody murder or jumps out of bed to come running after you, calmly and lovingly return him to his bed, say good night again, and leave. If a child can engage you in an extra snuggle, a shouting match, a third glass of water, or another bedtime story, he's won, and the battle will go on forever.

If he continues to cry, go back every ten minutes or so to reassure him that you're still there. But don't let him out of bed or engage him in any playing or talking. Pat him gently and lovingly on the back, say good night, and leave. In the beginning, you may have to take your child back to bed a dozen times, but if you're calm and persistent, eventually he'll learn that it's safe to go to sleep on his own.

If you have a child who is a night owl, you can't force him to go to sleep, but you can enforce the time by which he must be in bed. He can play quietly with a night light on until he falls asleep.

Bedtime is a wonderful time to share the day's happenings with your children, to enjoy bedtime stories and quiet moments without interruptions, and to teach them to reflect on the day's events and on life in general. And it's a great opportunity for you to see the world through their eyes. Creating a simple routine your kids look forward to will make bedtime more enjoyable for all of you.

6.

Make Storytime Special

"ONCE UPON A TIME, in a land far away . . ." How many images this simple phrase conjures up: memories of stories often told, exotic possibilities for new and exciting adventures, familiar characters like fairy princesses or fiery dragons, distant lands, rolling seas, and the animated faces and voices of our storytellers.

Some of my fondest recollections are the bedtime stories my dad used to tell us after lights out. Tucked warmly in bed, safe against the goblins of the night, nestled with a loving parent, we listened intently while adventures unfolded before us.

When Vera was little, her mother read Rudyard Kipling's *Rikki-Tikki-Tavi* to her and her brother. A chapter each night gave them a glimpse into the lives of an English boy and a mongoose confronted by a pair of evil cobras. Vera still vividly recalls how eagerly she looked forward to bedtime so she could find out what happened next.

If your parents read to you or told you stories at bedtime, these may constitute some of your most treasured childhood memories as well.

We remember these stories so clearly because of the richness of the experience. These are the kinds of memories we want to give our kids—quiet, loving moments together; stories that spark their imaginations and will stay with them forever.

Recent research has shown how much a child benefits—intellectually, emotionally, and developmentally—from being read to from an early age. We now know you can begin reading books to babies when they're newborn infants. There are special plastic books with colorful pictures that babies love to look at, or chew on—depending on their mood. Before they can talk, ask them to point to different things in the pictures. Later on, ask them to tell you about the illustrations.

When kids are a year old or so, you can read big picture books together. By the time they're toddlers you can begin making special excursions to the library to let them pick out the books they want you to read to them.

If you're not sure what books are appropriate for your child's age, ask your librarian. He or she will likely have a long list of suitable titles to choose from.

And don't forget to tell your kids bedtime stories about your own personal experiences, travels, or family history. Tell them a silly story about when they were babies. Or make up a story. Kids love it when the description of the main character sounds exactly like them.

Tell them a story about their day or their week, and include their friends in the tale. Tell them stories about the lives of their toys, dolls, and stuffed animals before they got "domesticated" and came to live in your house. Tell them tales about the wonderful things these characters do at night, after everyone else has gone to sleep.

Make up a fictional character or creature, and let your kids take turns telling the story. Let them decide what happens next.

Make the stories fun and enchanting, and leave them with just a bit of anticipation for the next installment. Bedtime is much simpler when kids can't wait to get to bed to find out what happens next.

The important thing from your children's point of view is the intimacy bedtime stories create—you're paying undivided attention to them. You're teaching them and soothing them with your voice and your presence. Don't rush. Don't make it a reading lesson, and don't grumble because it's interfering with the evening news or keeping you from the work you brought home from the office.

The years of snuggling at bedtime are very limited—before you know it, your kids decide that they're too old for stories and bedtime hugs, so take advantage of every cuddly moment.

7.

Free Your Weekends for Your Family

A WORKING MOTHER with a seven-year-old son recently told me about her experiences with simplifying. She'd been intrigued by the idea of living more simply, but it seemed an impossible goal. She was self-employed, worked long hours, and had very little free time.

Then one day her son asked her, "Mommy, do you ever sit down?"

She was stunned by his question, but she knew immediately what he meant: Her schedule was so hectic that she was always running from one task to another, never taking the time to simply sit and be with him. After giving it some serious thought, she decided that while she couldn't figure out how to reduce her work week for the time being, she *could* simplify her weekends.

So, bit by bit, she adjusted her schedule. Now from five P.M. on Friday until nine A.M. on Monday she takes no phone calls; she makes no phone calls; she accepts no social invitations; she doesn't read the newspapers or watch TV; and she runs no errands—if they don't get run during the week, they don't get done.

She spends the entire weekend with her husband and son. They have lazy mornings sleeping in, reading, and playing games together. They may go for a walk or see a movie, but they don't schedule anything they *have* to do. Her friends know that unless it's an emergency she's simply not available on the weekend.

By Monday morning she's not only had hours of uninterrupted time with her family, but she's rested and ready to start another hectic week.

Perhaps, because of the ages of your children or other family obligations you might have, it's not possible for you to simplify your entire weekend right now. But think of some ways you could free up part of it, or another part of your week.

I heard from one reader, a physician with a part-time family practice who, along with her husband and their four kids—twelve to sixteen—make Friday their "Sandwich and Movie Night." They have sandwiches, and their once-a-week indulgence of chips, while they all relax and wind down from the week by watching a video together.

8.

Take Time for Yourself

IT'S IMPORTANT to be realistic about the amount of time it takes to raise happy, healthy kids. You may already have come to terms with the fact that, especially while your kids are young, there are many things you might like to do that you simply won't have the time to do right now.

But you'll need to learn to take *some* time for yourself. It's so easy to fall into the habit of gearing your whole life and all your energies to your kids. While they certainly should be the primary focus of your attention, they should not be your only focus. That's not healthy for you or your kids.

Make sure you arrange your schedule so you can take time for yourself each day—and each week. This is especially true if you're the primary caregiver. If you don't take some time on your own, you'll be exhausted, resentful, and unable to provide clear guidance and direction for your kids. You have to learn to take care of yourself in order to be able to care happily for the rest of your family.

Here are some ideas on how to get the time you need.

Find a small calendar that has—or on which you can indicate—hourly increments. For the next couple of weeks, keep close track of how you spend your time throughout the day. Then figure out what you could stop doing and still survive.

Things you eliminate might include: staying later at the office than you actually need to; shopping in the mall or browsing at garage sales; unnecessary chauffering and errand running; idle telephone conversations; watching television; perusing magazines and junk mail; excessive laundering and housekeeping; unnecessary and unproductive meetings. Drop what you can and change your schedule accordingly.

Schedule time for yourself from the very beginning. Sit down each week with your spouse and your family calendar (#76). Figure out when you can take some time on your own, and write it in on the calendar. Schedule your time off at the same time each day and each week so you—and your family—get into the habit of it.

If you don't put it on the schedule, something will always come up, and you won't take the time. Then, as the days, weeks, and months pass, it gets more and more difficult to take even a short time away. Your family expects you to always be there, and you begin to worry about leaving your kids with anyone else.

Possibly the greatest challenge is to take time for yourself when you're nursing a baby, especially in those first few months. It's especially challenging when you've got another child or two besides the nursing infant. Vera finally learned—with her third child—to nap when the baby napped. Exhaustion haunted the early years with her first two children; she was determined that wouldn't happen with her third child. She simply arranged her life so that the older kids could either be under someone else's supervision or could quietly occupy themselves until she and the baby woke up.

But even when her first two kids were young, Vera took Saturday afternoons for herself by arranging to leave Peter and Sasha with Tim. This provided a break for her, and it was good for Tim and the kids. The children learned to separate from their mother in a safe environment, and to see that it was okay to allow someone else to meet their needs. Tim began to appreciate what parenting was all about on those Saturday afternoons, and he grew to value this time alone with his kids.

Don't underestimate the benefits you can get from taking even five minutes several times throughout the day to stop and rest. Deep, deep, deep breathing for a couple of minutes helps too, as does stepping out into the sunshine for a bit and simply basking in the light and the fresh air.

Staying hydrated also relieves fatigue, so when you're feeling tired drinking a tall glass of water will help revitalize you.

One way to get time on a daily basis is to use the quiet period in the evening after the rest of the family has gone to bed. Tim and Vera have time together after 9:30, when their kids are all tucked in. Tim goes to bed by ten; Vera goes to bed around eleven-thirty. That gives Vera a peaceful hour and a half on her own to catch up on her reading, to do some writing, or to make telephone calls in peace. She's a night owl, so this works for her.

If you're a morning person, get up earlier than everyone else in the house—having even half an hour to drink a cup of tea in solitude will make a difference. Don't give in to the temptation to use this time for chores or busywork; you can do those things while the kids are awake, noisy, and demanding. This is quiet time for you to do things that will restore your psyche and your soul.

It's possible you've been so busy and worn out since having kids that you've forgotten what those things are. So take some of your quiet time to figure out what you've been missing: reading, napping, taking walks, gardening, exercising, or visiting with a friend.

And while you're at it, be sure to schedule time each week when you and your spouse can be together, without the kids. My friends Tamara and Bill have done this since their two boys were babies. They've made Thursday evening their night out, and they allow nothing to interfere with this time.

Tamara tells me the key to being able to do this is that they've had a standing order with the same sitter for years. This way they, their kids, and the sitter all expect it and can plan for it. And they don't fall into the habit of having to cancel—and eventually stop taking that time—because they couldn't find someone to stay with the kids.

Taking time for yourself and for each other is important not only for your own health and self-esteem, it's also an important example to set for your kids.

Two
THE WORKLOAD

9.

Simplify the Household Routines

ASK MOST HARRIED PARENTS what their biggest household headaches are and you'll hear complaints about frustrating attempts to keep the house in order and get the laundry done. Both take time and energy that most people would rather devote to other things. How do you simplify these inescapable tasks?

You can start by lowering your standards. It's nice to have a neat house, but it doesn't always have to be immaculate. It's okay if the beds don't get made every day and if you don't change the sheets every week. Clean what's dirty, but go for lived-in rather than spotless.

Keep a broom and dustpan and a sponge handy for small messes, and teach your kids to clean up their own spills and mishaps, even when they're very young and need a little help from you.

By the time they're seven you can show your kids where the vacuum cleaner is and how it works. Put vacuuming their own rooms on the chores list—but teach them to pick up their LEGO and other small toys *before* they turn on the vacuum cleaner.

Teach your kids to be responsible for their own things (#32).

Every night before bedtime, have them go through the house, collect their belongings, and put them away.

If possible, restrict toys to the kids' rooms and the family room. If you allow toys in other areas of the house, keep baskets or toy chests nearby for easy storage.

Limit the amount of clothes each member of the family has (#21), and teach everyone to wear them longer. Wash clothes when they're dirty instead of after every time they're worn. Jeans can usually be worn more than once before they get washed, as can outer clothes like sweatshirts or sweaters.

Do the laundry on a routine basis rather than haphazardly. Once a week is a good goal to shoot for. Avoid traffic jams in the laundry room by assigning a different day to each kid who does his own laundry.

Give every member of the family two zippered mesh bags to keep in their sock drawer—one for clean socks, the other for dirty ones. When the socks come off at the end of the day, they go into the dirty-sock bag, which gets washed and dried on laundry day with the socks in it. It then goes directly into the sock drawer and becomes the clean sock bag. (If there are any clean socks left over from the previous week, transfer them to the *new* clean sock bag.) No more sorting, matching, or losing socks, or wondering who they belong to.

These are minor steps, but they add up quickly in terms of the time and energy they'll save you.

10.

Share the Workload

In addition to having your kids take care of their clothes and personal belongings, you can greatly simplify your life by having your children help with the daily and weekly chores around the house.

Routine jobs can be listed on a chart, which is posted for easy reference. The chart becomes the chores enforcer. If a chore is listed there, it's not subject to debate or discussion. "It says right here it's Gabe's night to do the dishes." This removes the emotional component from getting your kids to pitch in. The more they help, the simpler it is for you.

Attach your chores list to the front of the fridge or to a kitchen bulletin board. Divide the tasks between the kids. At dinnertime, for example, one child empties the dishwasher and sets the table; the other clears the table, rinses the dishes, and stacks the washer. Alternate assigned tasks according to their schedules. Other jobs—shoveling snow or washing the car—can be assigned on an as-needed basis.

Parents can trade off "policing" each night to make sure the kids have done their jobs. This way one parent doesn't always end up being the bad guy.

Have your kids share the workload from the time they're very young. Give them more responsibility as they get older and are able to do more. Don't expect perfection right away. Show them how you want things done, and praise their early efforts. Remember that it takes time to learn to do things right. A gentle suggestion is more helpful than impatient criticism.

By age seven or eight, children can straighten and clean their own rooms each week, put away their toys, and help with laundry. At the very least, they can take their dirty clothes to the laundry room at the end of the week or put them in a laundry bag. At best, they can wash their clothes themselves.

Peter has been washing, folding, and putting away his own laundry for the past several years. The key is having clothes that can all be washed together without colors running, and that don't need to be ironed. He's also responsible for mowing the lawn and helping with leaf removal.

Sasha loves to cook, and makes great chicken dumplings and chocolate chip cookies. If you give kids the opportunity—and the right-sized tools—they'll enjoy helping with everything from cleaning to organizing to pruning the trees.

Getting reluctant children involved is easy: The chores have to be done before they can do anything else, such as watch TV, have a friend over, start their homework, spend time on the phone, have story time, or get a ride to town. Be firm, and they'll have nothing else to do but that unfinished job.

Don't accept any excuses for chores undone or half done.

Many parents I hear from believe that household duties should come before schoolwork. I agree. Otherwise, kids use homework as an excuse to procrastinate with chores. Contributing to the family is as important a lesson as whatever they're learning at school.

Kids need to learn to schedule time for homework *and* housework. Of course, you can always make exceptions before an important exam or when they're loaded down with homework. But the whole process will work much more smoothly if chores have to be done before they do anything else.

If your kids have never been required to help around the house, your task will be more challenging. But remember, it's never too late to start making requests. Sit down with your kids and explain why every family member needs to pitch in and help. Don't forget, you're the parent (#50). You have the right to expect that your reasonable requests will be honored.

11.

Create Easy-to-Follow House Rules

ONE THING that makes life complicated for many parents is that they fall into the pattern of reacting to their kids' behavior, rather than making it clear how they want their kids to behave. Instead of requesting that a child never slam the door, for example, parents often spend their energy yelling at the kids every time the door gets slammed.

After a while, a child turns a deaf ear to the parent, or gets upset because he's tired of being yelled at. Or the parent explodes because he's tired of yelling at the kids and getting no change in their behavior. Creating some easy-to-follow house rules will help solve this problem.

Take some time to come up with few rules that would make life simpler for your family. Be sure to explain a new rule to your kids before the offending behavior becomes a habit.

Here are some house rules you might want to consider. Obviously, you don't have to use all of them. Take any one or a combination that might apply to your household, or add a couple of these to your own list:

1. When you use a dish, rinse it and put it in the dishwasher.
2. When you take something out of the refrigerator, the cupboard, a drawer, or the toolbox, put it back where it belongs when you're finished with it.
3. When you create garbage or trash, dispose of it in the appropriate manner: put it in the garbage can or disposal, the compost bin, the recycling boxes, or a wastebasket.
4. Wipe off the counters after you've used them.
5. You can eat only in the kitchen, the dining room, or outside. Every other room is off limits.
6. Ask permission before you borrow something that belongs to someone else. Return it in the same condition in which you found it. If you break it, fess up.
7. Bathroom time is private time. Whatever you have to say to someone who's in the bathroom can wait until the person comes out.
8. Don't yell across rooms when you need to talk to someone. Go to where the person is and talk.
9. Close—don't slam—outside doors behind you as you come in and go out of the house.
10. Turn off the lights, the TV, the stereo, and the CD player when you're not using them.
11. Take your dirty or wet shoes off outside before coming into the house.

12. Hang up your coat or jacket when you come in. (Have coat trees or hooks children can reach so they can do it on their own.)
13. Tiptoe around anyone who's sleeping. Never wake her up.
14. Don't bother anyone doing his homework.
15. Unless the house is on fire, don't interrupt anyone who's on the phone.
16. Never, ever remove the pen that sits next to the phone pad.

In the beginning your kids will no doubt need to be gently reminded about a house rule over and over again: "Peter, put the peanut butter back in the fridge, please." Then one day you'll discover to your amazement that a child has actually incorporated a rule into his routine.

One easy way to get your kids to follow your house rules is to start when they're very young—and continue through their teenage years—acknowledging their accomplishments by sincerely and enthusiastically *describing* their behavior to them, even their smallest achievements: "Wow! You turned off the lights!" "Gee, you wiped off the countertop!" "You didn't interrupt me the whole time I was on the phone!"

It sounds so basic, but it shows them you're paying attention, and often they'll try even harder to follow the rules. Loving encouragement is one of the most important aspects of child rearing, and using it liberally will simplify many areas of your life with kids.

And, of course, a good way to instill rules of any type is by your quiet example.

Your house rules will constantly be evolving; they'll change as your kids grow and as old rules become habits or are discarded. New rules will emerge to handle new situations, such as when your sixteen-year-old starts getting family car privileges and leaves her jacket, gym bag, and schoolbooks all over the back seat. The new rule might be: Before you return the keys to the car, clean out your personal belongings.

Make sure your kids understand that your house rules also apply to any friends they bring home. If you find a mess on your kitchen table created by your child and her guest, insist that they work together to clean it up. Your child's friends—who may not have the same house rules you do—have to respect your home and its rules or they don't get invited back.

Household rules and courtesies may seem elementary to you, but they have to be taught to kids. Once they become established as habits in each member of the household, your family life will be immeasurably simpler.

12.

Learn to Do One Thing at a Time

ONE OF THE SKILLS that come with parenting is the seemingly innate ability to do a dozen things at a time. We think this makes it possible for us to get more done than we would otherwise, and it does—up to a point. But many parents have long since passed that point, and then doing too many things at once creates more problems than it solves.

Take some time right now to think about the number of times throughout the day you try to do too much, and then spend some time thinking about how you might begin to do things differently.

The next time you spill your coffee while you're driving to work in the morning, pull off the road to clean up the mess. Avoid attempting to drive with one hand while frantically cleaning up the car, your child, and yourself with the other. Better yet, don't drink coffee (or anything else) while you're driving—it only complicates your life. Instead, get up early enough to have your coffee at home.

The next time you find yourself preparing dinner while holding a fussy child, don't answer the phone when it rings. Let the answering machine pick it up. If it's your son needing a ride home, then you can pick it up. And if call waiting beeps while you're making arrangements with your son, ignore it—you're on the most important call right now; everything else can wait until later.

The next time you find yourself reading a magazine while you're watching TV and attempting to carry on a conversation with your mate, in between helping your child with her homework and waiting for the timer to go off for the cookies you promised to bake for your daughter's class the next day, stop. Set the magazine aside. Move away from the TV. If you don't have time to read your magazines, cancel your subscriptions until you can create the time—that's one less mound of clutter and one less distraction you'll have to deal with. If your child regularly needs help with her homework, set aside some time each day when you can give her your undivided attention.

And the next time you find yourself tempted to volunteer to make a salad for thirty people, build a set for the school play, or submit a report on the financial status of any organization, stop. Bite your tongue, sit on your hands, look intently out the window, leave the room quietly, or say no thank you and hang up quickly. Do whatever you have to do to keep yourself from committing to one more task you don't have time for and that will take your energies away from your family.

This is not to say you should never volunteer. In fact, as you simplify your life and free up more time for yourself and your family, volunteering may become an important part of your family's life. And certainly teaching your kids to volunteer (#80) will be a valuable contribution you can make to them. But you—and they—will be learning to give meaningfully from the heart. And you'll be able to free yourself from the sense of panic you get when you're trying to do it all.

You don't have to solve all the problems of the world today—there'll be time for that later. Keep remembering that the greatest contribution you can possibly make is to raise happy, healthy kids who know, by your example, how to create joy, satisfaction, and balance in their lives. Training yourself to cut back to doing one or possibly only two or three things at a time is a good place to start.

13.

Stop Trying to Do It All

ONE OF THE REASONS we end up doing too many things at one time is that we're trying to do it all. Not long ago I met a single mom with three sons, ages nine, thirteen, and sixteen. Her kids are polite and well behaved. She works full-time, her house is reasonably orderly, and she appears to have her life together.

I asked her how she did it all.

She said, quite frankly, "I *don't* do it all. I don't even try. I work full-time, and I spend the rest of the time with my kids. Period. I don't bake for anyone but the boys. I don't accept social invitations unless the kids are invited too and we all really want to go. My kids are my top priority right now; everything else has to wait. And I'm okay with that."

Her kids can't do all the things their friends do because money is tight, and she's not there after school to chauffeur them around. But she sees this as a good thing. Each of her kids is involved in a sports activity he likes, and the rest of their time is spent on schoolwork, playing with each other or the neighborhood kids, and having quiet time, which she has taught them how to enjoy (#81).

They watch only minimal amounts of TV, and it helps a lot that she lives in a neighborhood where there are several stay-at-home parents who are happy to keep an eye on each other's kids (#14).

She feels one of her biggest personal achievements has been developing the ability to move beyond the societal expectations of the so-called Super Mom. She sees the biggest advantage she has is that she knows she can't do it all, while many of the other people in her situation haven't figured that out yet, and are still wearing themselves out trying.

Whether you're a single working parent, part of a working couple, or a work-from-home or stay-at-home parent, the pressure to do it all is enormous. One basic way to simplify your life is learning to discriminate between the essential and the nonessential.

So figure out what your top two or three priorities are, spend your time and energy on them, and let the rest go. Simply accept that it's not possible to do it all, and that it's all right if you don't—in fact, it's immeasurably better if you don't. You can have a happy and fulfilling life while doing only part of it. People have done that successfully for years.

14.

Take All the Help You Can Get

HELP COMES in various forms when you're raising a family, and you can lighten your load considerably by learning to take advantage of whatever assistance is available as you need it.

A network of family, neighbors, and friends with children is a valuable asset. You can find out about children's play groups, classes, and activities from this network, as well as the names of the best baby-sitters, pediatricians, dentists, teachers, plumbers, electricians, carpenters, painters, and public services in your area.

You can commiserate, reassure, and advise each other. When you have a baby-sitting emergency, there'll almost always be someone to watch your child. And if you want to reduce the amount of time you spend in your car, you can carpool.

You don't have to be best friends with the other members of the group in order to tap into this resource. If you have kids on the same soccer team, that's reason enough to form a network.

Don't be shy about asking for help. Many parents hesitate to ask because they feel they're imposing, but people are usually delighted to oblige. Helping gives you a sense of being able to make a contribution to someone else. And you know there'll always be someone who'll return the favor when you need it.

Help is given from the heart, so don't keep score. It may not always be convenient to lend a hand, so don't take it as a personal affront if one of your requests is turned down. And remember, you're allowed to say no, too.

When you're dealing with friends and favors, be especially diligent about being punctual and doing what you say you will. It'll jeopardize your support network if people can't rely on you.

If you can afford paid help, arrange for it. And if you think you can't afford it, think again. When Vera and Tim were a struggling young couple with two small children, it cost fifty dollars a week to have the house cleaned, and Vera felt she couldn't afford cleaning help. She spent roughly eight hours a week cleaning the house and doing the laundry.

But then she realized that with her teaching background she could give French lessons for the going rate of twenty-five dollars an hour. After two hours of lessons, which she enjoyed, she could afford eight hours of housecleaning, which she abhors. The net result of this exchange was a clean house, clean laundry, and extra time each week to spend with her kids.

Take a close look at any talents you have that you can trade for help you may need.

A high school baby-sitter who comes on a regular basis is a

good source of relief. Or think about hiring a ten- to twelve-year-old baby-sitter to play with your baby or small child while you're at home, so you can have a couple of hours to yourself to read a book, have a quiet bath, or take a nap.

A live-in nanny can be great if cost is no object, if you don't mind giving up your privacy, and if you're a gambler. Having live-in help is a real challenge, though, and in my experience only rarely works well. According to my informal poll, the odds are about one in seven that you get someone who really clicks. It may simplify one area of your life while complicating many others; it's often more trouble than it's worth.

If you and your spouse both work, or if you're a single parent, consider getting day help for your kids. In this way, you can make sure your kids are cared for, and you can maintain your privacy.

But if you work from home, getting help with housework is easier and makes more sense, because it frees you to be with your kids. You can hire someone for just one or two chores, such as the laundry or yard work. Or you can get help for all the household duties.

Be creative. I heard from one mother who was trying to figure out how she could be in two places at once to pick up her kids. They live in a small town, and she finally realized there was no reason her children couldn't take a taxi if she couldn't be there to meet them.

Not only did this solve the immediate problem of transportation, but it gave her kids the experience of learning to deal with a cab in a safe environment. It also added to their sense of independence and their ability to take care of themselves. And it freed her from that "How am I going to pull *that* off?" feeling whenever she's confronted with a logistical conflict. This is obviously not an option for very young kids, and you'll want to make sure your child is comfortable with this arrangement.

If you're unable to establish a network of family and friends, look into state or federal or volunteer-sponsored programs such as Big Brothers/Big Sisters, the Mentor Project, Primary Intervention Programs (PIP), or any locally funded child services activities that provide assistance or guidance on either a short- or long-term basis.

Many communities have adult-supervised after-school programs so kids don't have to go home to an empty house. Check these out to see if you can get the help you need.

Three

THE STUFF

15.

Your Mother Didn't Need All That Stuff; You Don't Need It Either

MY PARENTS raised three kids with a crib, a playpen, and a high chair. Your parents may not have had a whole lot more than that, but many couples today feel they have to buy out the baby store in order to be good parents.

When Peter was a baby, Tim and Vera made the classic mistake of getting him *everything*. They slept on a hand-me-down bed with broken springs, but Peter had an antique cradle, and then a six-hundred-dollar crib with a built-in changing table, which later converted into a toddler bed.

Tim and Vera were barely scraping together their monthly car payments, but Peter had an infant car seat, then a bigger car seat, then finally a booster seat. He also had a carriage that converted into a stroller, a lightweight umbrella stroller, plus a backpack, a Snuggli, and a baby sling. They were suckers for any baby paraphernalia that looked appealing, as it all does, and it put them into credit-card debt for years to come.

At the time, they rationalized their purchases because they were planning to have another child. And they did use many of the same things when Sasha came along—though in the meantime they had to find a place to store them. But, as Vera admits, they didn't need it all, and they certainly didn't need to buy it all new. Eventually they had to sort through it, organize it, sell it, or give or throw it all away.

Seven years later, after they'd gotten rid of everything but the antique cradle, Andrew was born. They were better off financially than when their first two were babies, but they were also much wiser. They decided to do things differently.

They bought a one-hundred-fifty-dollar crib and one all-purpose stroller at a consignment shop—and paid cash. Then they borrowed the rest—high chair, playpen, walker, toddler bed, and car seats.

Vera and Tim had everything they needed for Andrew, and they had a couple thousand dollars or more in their bank account that they could apply toward a vacation or college fund—or toward that old credit-card debt from Peter's babyhood.

It's unrealistic to expect that you can get everything that's out there for your child, or to feel that you should. So avoid the temptation to buy all those adorable things you think you'd like to have, and focus on what you need.

Essentials might include a crib, a stroller, a car seat, a high chair, and an infant seat. Convenient, but not absolutely necessary, are a cradle (you can use a crib) and a changing table (why not use a bed?). Or cover a bureau top with a foam cushion—it can be converted back to a bureau when the time comes, and you won't have a changing table to get rid of.

Borrow or buy from consignment shops those items you decide you need for a short while. Most people are tired of storing baby things and are only too happy to recycle them.

There may be other items you might require, such as a jogging stroller if you're a committed jogger. But remember, unless you learn to discriminate between what you actually need and what advertisers would like you to believe you need, you're likely to end up with a lot of things that will only complicate your life.

16.

Keep the Kids' Toys to a Minimum

IN ADDITION TO everything we feel we must have to take care of our kids, we also allow our kids to have too much in the way of toys, clothes, bikes, skis, roller skates, books, pets, games, electronic gear—the list is endless.

Toys are probably the biggest issue. Some toys can be a blessing—they can keep your children happily occupied for hours on end, and the good ones can even be instructive.

But toys can be the bane of your existence as they get lost, get broken, or get stepped on—barefoot—in the middle of the night. Toys are the source of most squabbles between siblings, and if you don't keep them under control, toys can quickly overrun your house, your garage, your driveway, and your yard.

So what's the simplest way to win the toy wars? The first line of defense is to minimize the number of toys your kids own. Limit your toy purchases to Christmas, your kids' birthdays, and special occasions. Otherwise, no new toys. When the kids find something they want, have them put it on their birthday or Christmas wish list.

The second line of defense is to set limits on gifts from family and friends. Don't be afraid to draw the line with doting relatives on the number of gifts they give your kids. Consider setting up a vacation or a college fund that loving grandparents can contribute to. Or ask for "experience" gifts: a day at the zoo or the nature center, a week at summer camp, or a matinee performance of a classic children's play or concert.

Realize that your kids don't have to have the latest toy that comes along. Avoid video games, Ninja turtles, action figures, and other trendy, gimmicky items.

This also means supervising and limiting the amount of commercial television your kids watch and teaching them at an early age that they can't have every toy they see advertised on TV.

When you do buy toys, get durable ones that will last forever, that offer a variety of creative play possibilities, and that your child is really interested in. Choose toys that can grow into a collection, such as LEGO, Lincoln Logs, Brio trains, or dollhouse furniture. Toys like wooden blocks, Matchbox cars, dolls, and stuffed animals remain favorites with kids.

Toys that stimulate a child's imagination include costumes for dressing up; a paint set or felt-tip markers with lots of paper; traditional games like checkers, chess, or Scrabble. And, of course, you can get a lot of mileage from outdoor toys like tricycles, bikes, and swing sets.

Don't buy badly made toys even if they're at the top of your child's wish list—they break much too quickly, and will disappoint a hopeful child.

Your child doesn't need to own every toy his friends have. When Peter was young, Vera—still in the overdoing it mode—bought him all the toys he enjoyed at school or at a friend's house. He lost interest in them quickly because they were so available to him. She's done the opposite with Andrew, who now looks forward to going to school because there are toys there he doesn't have at home.

Then there are those big-ticket items kids acquire and then don't use. Be sure your child really likes to play the cello or ice hockey before you go out and spend the money setting her up.

Rent equipment for activities that kids engage in only once in a while or gear they'll quickly outgrow. Ski shops have special lease packages or buy-back plans for kids. Roller blades and ice skates can be rented for a minimal fee. When you rent, you get the stuff in great shape, use it, and can give it back without having to find storage space for it. And your kids never outgrow it.

Buying from consignment shops and baby exchange stores and using hand-me-downs are other ways to minimize stuff. You get it when your kids are ready for it, and give it back or pass it on when they're finished with it.

And with libraries and video rental stores, there's no reason to own so many children's books or videos. Children outgrow these as well, so unless they're classics or real favorites, rent or borrow from the library rather than buy.

17.

Get Rid of Things on a Regular Basis

HAVING LOTS OF STUFF means having to spend lots of time cleaning it, fixing it, and putting it away, then trying to figure out what to do with it when it's outgrown or forgotten. Sort through your kids' things on a regular basis and keep only what they actually use.

There are several approaches you can take to getting rid of the things your kids don't need. One is the Major Sweep approach. Vera recently completed a big sweep through Sasha's room. They took everything but the heavy pieces of furniture out of the room: everything in the closets and the bureau, all the toys and the books. Then Sasha put back only those items she still used.

Vera ended up with a stack of discarded clothes, toys, and books in the hallway, but Sasha's room was neat as a pin. The rejects were separated into hand-me-downs (one bag for her younger cousin, others for neighbors and friends); consignment shop articles; Goodwill pieces; and things that would go straight into the trash.

That very same day, Vera and Sasha carried the useless items straight to the bin. Everything else was loaded into the car for immediate delivery. The consignment shop was the first stop. Anything rejected there went directly to Goodwill. Then she passed on some of the hand-me-downs to friends, and mailed another box to her sister-in-law.

A project like this can take a whole day, so you need to schedule the appropriate amount of time and commit to seeing it through.

You can achieve the same results with the Minor Sweep approach. Put aside an hour or so every Saturday morning for the next few months. Pick a room. The first week clean out the dresser; the next week clean out the closet; and so on. You'll need to set aside some space, perhaps in the garage, as a holding area for the items you'll be adding each week as you tackle the next area of the room.

This is the challenging part—keeping all those throwaway piles around while you're still adding to them. It's so tempting, when you bring this week's castoffs out to the holding area, to pick up something you threw out last week and think, Gee, I might be able to use this someday, and bring it back into the house. Who hasn't done this? So, even though it's a duplication of effort, you might consider making a Goodwill or consignment shop run each week until you're through. For many people, out of sight, out of mind is crucial at this juncture.

A good rule of thumb when deciding what to get rid of is, if it hasn't been used or worn in a year, out it goes. But keep in mind that nothing interests a child more than a forgotten toy you're now ready to get rid of.

One way to handle this dilemma is to suggest the name of someone who might use it more than your children would; kids are sometimes more willing to give something away if they know where it's going. But if they're really adamant about keeping an item, let them play with it for a while. When you see they've lost interest in it again, put it aside. If they ask for it, then you'll know they still really do want it. If not, give it away with everything else.

Some other rules of thumb are: Don't keep broken toys. Don't keep unidentifiable parts of toys. Don't keep things you don't know what to do with. Don't move things from one closet to another. Don't keep things just in case your children might change their minds. If you plan to have another child, keep only the really good stuff: crib, high chair, playpen, and stroller.

Do the first clean-out as soon as you can. Then pick a natural break in the family schedule—when your kids finish school in the spring, or before they start back to school in the fall—and establish your Major or Minor Sweep as an annual or semiannual routine. Or you could make it a family ritual to take place the weekend after Christmas or on New Year's Day to make room for any new toys.

Whatever way you choose to clean up, include your children, and make it fun. They know what they play with and what part goes with what toy. And they have to be there so you can see if last year's snowsuit still fits.

But most importantly, these are their things, and they have to take charge of them. Teach your kids to take responsibility for keeping their own things in order, and make it easy for them to let go of what they no longer use.

18.

Don't Put It in the Attic (or in the Basement)

A FEW YEARS AGO Vera and Tim and their young family moved into the home where Vera and her brothers had grown up. They felt fortunate to have more room for their brood, but they ended up in a house with forty years' accumulation of things to sort through. It took months of weekends to clear out more than two tons of junk—mostly from the attic and basement—which went straight to the dump. So many other miscellaneous items remained that they held a tag sale and netted over three thousand dollars.

Many things had lived in the attic for so long they'd been completely forgotten. Some items that had been put away in good order were totally ruined, either by the dryness of the attic or by the humidity in the basement, and had to be tossed. Many treasures that had been put away for a younger child had already been outgrown. It was a nightmare that could have been avoided.

A good rule for attics and basements is that they be used *only* as a temporary holding space for seasonal items. If you have easy access to it, an attic is great for storing out-of-season clothes, toys (sleds, wading pools), sports equipment (skis, ice skates), Christmas decorations, and a limited number of hand-me-downs waiting for the next child. If access is difficult or dangerous, don't use it.

Basements, if they're dry, are good for cleaning and paint supplies, tools, and the winter storage of gardening tools, pots, and planters.

You know that anything stored in the garage soon becomes infested with cobwebs, silverfish, and roly-poly bug corpses. So use the garage only to house cars, bikes, neatly arranged and frequently used yard and garden equipment, and anything else that comes and goes on a regular basis, such as recyclables—cans, bottles, newspapers. Nothing else.

Don't use any of these places as a way station for things you might need someday or don't have room for in the house. If it's stored away, you obviously don't need it now; you probably won't be using it in the future; it'll be in the way of something you will need; you'll forget about it; and there's a good chance it'll get ruined. It's so much simpler to get it out of your house and out of your life.

Never store family archives or financial records in the attic, the basement, or the garage. Invest in a new or used filing cabinet or even a cardboard file box (with a lid) in which a small number of family heirlooms and financial records—categorized and clearly labeled—can be stored. This can be kept in the area where you pay the bills: in the kitchen, next to your desk, or in a convenient closet.

Unless you've got a complicated tax picture or a home-based business, tax records need to be kept for only three years. Each year, at the time you file your tax return, dispose of the four-year-old files you no longer need.

19.

What to Do with Baby Teeth, Pasta Paintings, and Other Keepsakes

EARLY ARTWORK AND WRITINGS, a lock of hair from their first haircut, photographs—these are legitimate memorabilia that you and your children might someday enjoy having. But you don't have to keep every drawing, every photograph, their tonsils, or their umbilical cord. Let the Tooth Fairy keep their baby teeth.

And perhaps there should be a special ruling on pasta paintings—the ones with noodles or beans glued to a piece of paper in the shape of a favorite Sesame Street character. Under this ruling, kids could do all the pasta paintings they want at school, but the finished product would stay in the classroom. At the very least, this would save you from having to sweep up Big Bird's tomato penne beak, which invariably falls off the minute your child comes through the front door.

Kids naturally want to save every work of art they create, and it's important that their talents be appreciated. But unless you have a system for dealing with these works, they can quickly take over the house.

One solution is to keep a cardboard file box in which you temporarily store all the artwork your kids do. As each piece is brought in, greet it with genuine and enthusiastic appraisals. Then, after a suitable viewing time—and possibly even a posting to the fridge or family bulletin board—make sure each piece is signed and dated by the artist, then carefully place it in this art box.

The art box is just the first step. It gives your children the feeling that you care about their work, and it avoids arguments over why you're throwing out the newly created Christmas tree painstakingly decorated with now-molting confetti.

Once or twice a year go through the box with your children. Decide together what stays and what goes. You might have a policy that you won't keep anything that was drawn or cut out by somebody else, that is made out of popsicle sticks, or that sheds angel dust, legumes, or pasta of any type.

By this time, the child is more detached from the work and is able to make choices about what to throw out and what to keep. These thoughtfully culled pieces can then be moved into a portfolio that becomes a part of the child's permanent collection, which might also include a baby book, birth certificate, report cards, graduation certificate, and any notes or records of achievement.

You might also want a box for each child that can hold other items such as clay figurines, a silver baby cup, or other things that don't fit into the portfolio. This container should be sturdy and about the size of a large shoe box. Each treasure is labeled or tagged with the date and the child's name.

Photographs are perhaps the most universal family souvenir, but they can be frustrating to deal with if they're not properly labeled. When you take pictures of your family, learn to go easy on the shutter button. When you get a packet of photos back from the developer, immediately and ruthlessly throw away the out-of-focus shots and the scenes where Uncle Ted is standing too close to the camera. Select the photos you'd like to frame, and put the rest back in the envelope, labeled with the date, the location, and a brief description of the occasion or the event.

Store the packets in an accessible location, such as a kitchen cabinet or a desk drawer, until you have time to put them in albums— one for the entire family, or one for each child. The final albums will be simple chronologies of your lives together, with dates, places, and names clearly marked on each photo. This can be a fun family project for a rainy weekend.

20.

Create an Easy Living Space for Your Kids

EVERYTHING in a child's room needs to be strong and functional. This is no place for an antique bureau or Aunt Harriet's hand-pieced quilt.

As we've already seen, for a baby's room you'll need a crib, a bureau, and maybe a changing table. That's about it.

When your child outgrows his crib, he'll need a sturdy bed. If you possibly can, get one that will take him through his teenage years. Bunk beds are ideal, and if two children share the room, they're great space savers. Be prepared with a futon or a convertible foam chair for nights they have company.

Kids need shelves for books, a desk or work space for schoolwork and art projects, and a bureau for folded clothes. Or, instead of a bureau, you can keep shelves or organizers in the closet so the kids can hang up their own clothes and easily dress themselves.

They also need a system for keeping their toys in order. Store each set of toys in its own clearly marked box. Large storage boxes with tops—the kind that neatly stack in the corner of the room—are good organizers. As noted earlier, if you don't confine toys to certain areas of the house, they'll take over. You might have a rule that your kids are allowed to play with their toys only in their bedrooms. A family room or rec room is also a good place for a toy center. Make the rest of the house off limits for toys.

Teach your kids to put their toys away when they've finished playing with them. Help them with cleanup when they're younger by giving them one manageable job at a time. They can stack all the wooden blocks, or put the stuffed animals back on the bed. Make it a game to spark their interest.

The less furniture there is in the room, the more floor space there is for playing.

If you want to keep life simple, never put a TV in a child's room. Not only will it clutter up her space—not to mention her mind—but it'll be harder to control what she watches.

As your children mature, their needs change and their rooms will adapt to their new interests. By keeping it simple, you don't spend money on furniture and accessories that children quickly outgrow.

21.

Simplify Your Kids' Wardrobes

CHILDREN'S CLOTHING requirements are very basic. They need everyday school clothes, play clothes, and a dress-up outfit. That's it. Don't go overboard buying cute little togs for your kids—they won't wear them often enough to justify the expense, the maintenance, or the space they take up in their closets.

Keep in mind how quickly kids outgrow clothes. Babies can grow a pound and an inch a month in their first year. Like toddlers, they require several changes of clothing a day because of the mess they make. But you really don't need more than seven or eight outfits in each size range—three months, six months, nine months, twelve months, eighteen months. Since kids grow so fast, make sure their clothes are appropriate for the season.

Get tops that have crotch snaps so the baby doesn't have a drafty tummy. Resist the temptation to buy those darling dresses for crawling baby girls—a dress hinders mobility because the child's knees get tangled up in the skirt.

Use pants with elastic waistbands that are easy to pull on and off for kids who are being potty trained. Kids in diapers need bottoms that have snaps up the legs.

Regardless of age, kids don't need more than eight or ten outfits a season: three or four pairs of pants or shorts and a dozen tops is plenty. Everything you buy should be machine-washable.

Kids need T-shirts, shorts, bathing suits, and sandals or sneakers in the summer and long pants with long-sleeved shirts and a couple of sweaters and sweatshirts for winter. For outer wear, they'll need a raincoat, a light jacket, perhaps a snowsuit or parka, and hat and gloves. Polarfleece—warm, good-looking, durable, layerable, machine-washable, and good anywhere—is a simple, cross-seasonal fabric for kids.

They'll also need sleepwear and underwear—and identical socks so they don't have to be matched—for each day of the week. A pair of rain/snow boots and possibly a pair of dress shoes will round out their clothing needs.

As your kids get older and start to develop their own opinions about fashion, the simplest way to buy their clothes is to take them with you so they can pick out what they like. Your job is to to make sure their clothes fit properly and to temper their more radical tastes.

It might be helpful to have a policy that both you and your child have to like something before you'll buy it. You don't want to impose your sense of style on kids, but as long as it's your money you get to decide whether they can have anything outrageously skimpy, overly baggy, or in the fluorescent family. Remember, you're the parent. If you veto something they feel they absolutely have to have, they can buy it with their own money.

Consignment shops and sales at a store like Gap Kids are good places to get value for your money. Or wait for seasonal sales at department stores.

Another easy way to involve your kids in the process of selecting their own clothes is to shop by mail order. Land's End and L. L. Bean, for example, offer practical, durable clothing for children.

One problem with shopping by mail is that the mail-order houses are relentless, sending out four to six catalogs a year. Not only do these quickly clutter up your home, they're a constant source of temptation to buy more than you actually need. So learn to be relentless yourself. Keep the number of houses you order from to a minimum, and recycle the catalogs as quickly as they arrive. Use the toll-free number to take your name off the mailing list when you no longer buy through a particular catalog.

Fashion swings, growth spurts, and your children's changing sense of style are reason enough never to buy clothes before you need them, even if they're on sale. It's a waste of time, money, and energy to buy a snowsuit in the spring when your child will outgrow it by winter. Girls go in and out of dresses, leggings, and pants phases quickly. And a child may love sweats one day and insist on wearing only blue jeans the next.

Never buy anything that needs ironing. Stick to matching color schemes so that everything goes with almost everything else and can be washed together.

22.

Teach Your Cat to Fetch

IF YOU REALLY WANT to simplify your life, think seriously before you acquire a pet.

When my friend Jamie's son Adam was two, she bought him a puppy, with the idea that the two of them could grow up together. A romantic notion, but the reality turned out to be much more complicated. It was twice as much work for Jamie because she now had two unruly creatures to manage instead of one.

A toddler doesn't know how to treat a dog properly, so unless you're well versed in dog-training techniques and have the time and the energy to train the dog and the child at the same time, you're better off waiting until the child is older.

But even when your child reaches a responsible age, a dog is not simple. By the time Adam was ten, he'd been begging for a puppy for years. Jamie finally relented and gave him a little Peke-a-poo, on the condition that he'd be responsible for the care of the dog. Adam has kept his part of the bargain: he feeds Jasmine, cleans up her messes, cuts her hair, picks out ticks, gives her flea baths, and loves her unconditionally.

But Jamie still has to schedule Jasmine's shots, take her to the vet, buy her food and treats, and generally supervise her care. She also had to deflea the house twice last year, and many of the kids' toys and several pieces of furniture have been ruined by Jasmine's chewing.

Over the last fifteen years Jamie has owned practically every kind of pet available, and she's pleased to be down to just Jasmine. If you're thinking about getting a pet for your child, you can benefit from Jamie's mistakes by considering her list of pets, from most difficult to easiest.

The most demanding pet to have is a dog. Dogs require more attention, training, grooming, and supervision than most other animals, and they suffer greatly when they don't get the attention they need. They're totally dependent on you, which is their attraction for some people. But having a dog is like having a child stuck at age three forever—charming, maybe, but lots of work.

Furry animals that live in cages are the next hardest. Contrary to popular opinion, rabbits, hamsters, mice, ferrets, guinea pigs, and gerbils are all difficult pets. Their cages need to be cleaned on a daily basis. If you skip a day or two, the stench is unbearable. Of course, you can keep the rabbit outside, but then he's forgotten. These pets don't sustain a child's interest over a long period of time, and they're not affectionate and don't form an attachment to their owners. A child can't really play with them, either, and they're always trying to escape—who can blame them?—and there's a strong possibility that your child or someone else's will be bitten.

Pet birds are tough, too, because unless they're trained—which takes a huge commitment of time and energy—they frequently want nothing to do with you. Their fluttering scatters feathers and seeds throughout the room, no matter how often you clean their cages. They're fragile and get sick easily, and all the feathers and seed dust can aggravate some respiratory ailments. Except for parrots, birds seldom become personally attached to their owners, so it's hard to become attached to them. And it's such a heartbreaker to see a caged bird, or a caged animal of any kind.

An aquarium seems like a simple way to satisfy the urge to keep a pet—until the fish start eating each other, or the heater malfunctions and you find them floating upside down in your expensive tank. There are so many factors to consider when setting up an aquarium that, unless you're totally dedicated to doing it right, it won't live up to your expectations of ease or pleasure.

Fish can teach your child about disappointment and death, but these are lessons they'll learn anyway without getting their hopes up over a new pet. Carnival goldfish, especially, tend to die within days of being brought home. You might want to teach your kids not to participate in games in which a poor fish is the prize—it's cruel to the animal and heartbreaking for the child.

Reptiles and amphibians that live in tanks are fairly easy, if you don't mind providing them with a meal that is still walking or crawling around on its own. But a child can't really play with a snake, a turtle, or a frog, and kids quickly lose interest in animals they can't play with.

The simplest pet is a cat. It starts out as a cute kitten that's fun to play with but can't get into too much trouble. Kittens and cats keep themselves clean, so unless you get a long-haired cat there's no grooming to worry about—though they still shed. And some cats like to sharpen their claws on furniture, which can be an expense and a nuisance. But even the youngest kitten knows how to use a litter box. Cats can be cared for easily by neighbors while you're away. They're seldom as interactive as dogs—most cats could probably fetch a stick, though few would deign to—but the reward is a cuddly, lovable, responsive pet that is relatively independent.

23.

Stop Buying More Stuff

THE URGE TO KEEP buying more stuff often seems overwhelming. Carefully researched marketing campaigns are designed to make you feel guilty or somehow deprived if you don't have it all. Product advertising convinces you that if you get this one last thing, your children will finally be satisfied, and all your problems with your kids will be solved.

But invariably that one more thing adds little to your well-being and a lot to the clutter, the debt, and the confusion in your lives. Life becomes much simpler when you limit the acquisition of stuff.

In addition to training yourselves, you have to teach your kids early on that they can't have everything they want or think they want. How many times have you bought something your child desperately wanted—only to have her lose interest in it a couple of days later? How much of what the kids have now do they actually use? What would they miss? Probably not much.

Keep a list of things your kids need and go shopping only when you have something specific to buy. Never browse or window-shop. That's how impulse purchases are made.

Never buy anything you didn't know you needed until you saw it in the store window.

If you find something you think your kids absolutely have to have, put it on hold for a couple of days. Most likely you and they will forget about it.

Don't shop for anything but groceries for a period of a week or two, or even a month. You'll be amazed at the time and money you save. This is time you can spend with your kids, and money you can set aside for more important things.

Be realistic about what your kids actually need. Children have survived for centuries with a fraction of what's available today. What kids require more than anything else is lots of love and uninterrupted time with their parents. Those are the greatest gifts. Much of the other stuff just confuses the issue.

Four

THE PLUGGED-IN FAMILY

24.

Avoid Electronic Overload

ADVANCES IN TECHNOLOGY can either simplify or complicate our lives, depending on how we use them. As parents, it's our job to determine which of these are useful and desirable and to make some rational decisions as to what we allow our kids to have.

Here are some questions to ask yourself when you're thinking of buying the latest technological marvel for your kids: Is it educational? Does it add anything of quality to their lives? Will it isolate them from family and friends? Do they really need it? Can we acquire it without going into debt?

And here is a partial list of electronic gadgets that compete for our money and for our children's time and attention, along with some thoughts on how they can add to or detract from our lives.

Walkmans: The advantage of Walkmans is that they're inexpensive, they can be helpful in keeping your kids occupied with music or books-on-tape during long car trips, and kids can listen to their favorite music without bothering anyone else. But if they're overused they can be very isolating and can foster antisocial behavior.

If you allow your kids to have a Walkman, set some rules for their use of it. Don't permit them to use a Walkman at the dinner table, when doing their homework, while engaged in any form of conversation, when they're being introduced to your friends, or during any kind of social gathering. Don't let your kids wear them while riding a bike or rollerblading, when they won't be able to hear a car horn or other danger signals.

Stereos: Music is an important part of our lives. We know that children exposed to classical music learn more quickly in all areas of their lives than children who are not. Having one efficiently wired stereo system, which is sufficient for most homes, will make it possible for you to introduce your kids to all different types of music—classical, folk, rock and roll, reggae, Broadway musicals, and film scores.

You can make listening to music a family activity and an alternative to television. If your children want access to music in their rooms, they can use a Walkman with headphones. If they want something more sophisticated as they get older and develop their own musical preferences, they can buy it themselves with their allowance (#34).

Video games: Many parents I talk to have determined that this is one piece of electronic gear they won't allow their kids to own. Yes, kids love them, and they do keep kids occupied for long stretches of time. But so what? Apart from the time they waste, they're extremely addictive. Wouldn't you rather have your child spend the same time and energy reading, drawing, or learning to play a musical instrument?

If you already own video games, limit the time your kids spend playing with them, just as you would limit their exposure to television (#25).

Computer games: Some computer games are educational, intriguing, and challenging, and some consist of the same mindless rubbish you find on typical hand-held video games. You have to preview each game to see if there's anything of value to your kids.

Just as you do with television and video games, set some parameters on the time your children spend on computer games. Some kids won't stop playing until they're physically pulled away from the screen and the joystick is wrested from their clenched fists. Take away the game if your child won't abide by your rules.

Also, be sure you provide a balance by teaching your kids from an early age to enjoy quiet time (#81). Encourage them to get in touch with their own thoughts and creative ideas rather than having to be constantly plugged into someone else's noise.

25.

Set Television Rules

I'VE HEARD FROM MANY PARENTS who've reported that the best step they've taken to simplify their lives with kids is to get rid of the television altogether. While this is a plan I heartily recommend for simplifying anyone's life, I realize it's not a desirable option for many families.

Television programming includes stirring historical documentaries, superb dramatizations of classical books and plays, and informative science and nature programs. It also includes violence, insipid talk shows, and abysmal sitcoms about families of little interest to anyone.

It's your job as a parent to guide your children through this maze of glitter and grime, to select programs that will instruct, enlighten, and illuminate their world, and to steer them away from shows that are cynical, violent, stupid, scary, or tasteless.

The simplest way to do this is to set clear rules for your children about how much TV they can watch, when they can watch it, and which shows are permitted. Then stick to your policy no matter how many tears are shed, no matter how many voices are raised in protest. You've got the power of the plug. You can remove the television whenever you want to.

Insist that homework and chores be done before the TV is turned on. Have your kids ask to see a specific program, rather than just "watch TV." Don't allow *any* channel surfing, which usually means watching the best of the bad shows that are on at any given moment.

Establish limits that work for your family. I've heard from parents who allow no television during the week, and only a limited time for parentally approved programs—say two hours—per weekend.

If you allow your kids to watch TV, encourage them to tune in to educational shows and movies when they're available, or rent National Geographic or other nature videos. Good comedies can be a lot of fun, and they offer an opportunity for the entire family to laugh together.

It's easier to police TV viewing when you have only one set in the house.

Make it clear to any baby-sitters you hire that they cannot use the TV to keep the kids quiet while you're gone.

Watch TV with your kids occasionally so you know what they're watching and can answer questions they might have. Or use an appropriate program as a basis for further discussion or research. Encourage your kids to watch commercial-free public television programs. They'll see interesting and informative shows without being exposed to tempting toy ads.

Keep in mind that television can affect children in adverse ways that will complicate your life. Aggressive behavior, difficulty falling asleep, nightmares, and an insatiable appetite for advertised products can all be attributed to too much TV viewing or the wrong kinds of shows.

Even if you're closely monitoring the shows your children watch, sometimes a glimpse of the evening news or a violent preview for an upcoming show is enough to unsettle a young or sensitive child. If your kids are showing signs of agitation or sleep disturbances, try eliminating TV for a week or so to see if they improve.

Television viewing can be addictive, so if you're late getting started with setting rules, make an extra effort to provide other, more creative activities your children can become absorbed in.

As with many other areas of simplifying, the earlier in your kids' lives you establish these rules, the easier they'll be to enforce and maintain. And always remember that you're the parent.

Your kids will resist your efforts to limit their TV time. Discuss the reasons for your policies, but stick to your guns. This is a battle for their brains and their souls. So much television programming is inappropriate for kids that you simply can't leave the decisions up to them.

There's a slim chance that channel blockers and the V-chip technology that is now developing, as well as potential TV rating systems, will make your job easier. But you'll still be the one responsible for monitoring your kids' use of television and the time they spend with it.

26.

Choose Your Phone Options Wisely

THE OPTIONS for phones seem unlimited: table phones, wall phones, cordless phones, cellular phones, car phones, multiple phone lines, plus call waiting and dozens of other service options such as conference calls, rollovers, call forwarding, and caller identification. Then there are answering machines, fax machines, computer modems, and, soon, small screens with computer capabilities called Smart Phones. What do you really need?

One telephone line with call waiting, extensions in frequently used rooms if you have a large house, an answering machine, and an inexpensive or free car phone with an inexpensive calling plan can easily meet most family communications needs.

A separate children's telephone line made some sense before call waiting. Now one line is sufficient if you teach your children to use call waiting properly. They need to know that your calls have priority over theirs—if a call comes in for you while they're on the phone, they must ring off so you can take your call, no matter who it is.

Don't make the mistake one reader made. She had a separate

phone line installed in her sixteen-year-old daughter's room. She was tired of having the family line tied up forever when her daughter was on the phone. Then she realized she had lost control of the time this child spends on the phone—including calls late into the night. But even worse, most of the time she doesn't know who her daughter is talking to. A simpler plan would be to remember that she's the parent—then set some phone rules and stick to them. If her daughter doesn't abide by the rules, the logical consequence (#41) would be to remove the extra phone line.

One of the first things I did when I simplified my life was to drop call waiting from my phone service. I'm delighted to be rid of it—and the car phone—and regularly hear from readers who agree. But I've become convinced that if you have kids, call waiting and a car phone, if used within limits, can greatly simplify your life.

Call waiting is helpful because you can continue to make phone calls until the doctor calls back, or when you're expecting a child's request to be picked up after soccer practice. But remember, if you're in the middle of an urgent or important phone call, you don't *have* to pick up call waiting. If it's important, they'll call back.

An answering machine can be one of the greatest phone simplifiers, especially if you're the type who always runs to answer a ringing phone. Use the machine to pick up messages and screen calls when you're home, as well as to pick up messages when you're out. Learn to turn off the ringer on the phone and adjust the volume control on the answering machine during meals or when you don't want to be disturbed.

The car phone can be a real boon to parents. With a phone in your car, your kids can keep you informed of their activities, and you can call before you finally head for home to make sure everybody got off the bus and home okay. You can use the car phone to let your family know you've gotten delayed in traffic, what time you'll be home, and what they can do to get dinner started.

It's now possible to purchase an inexpensive cell phone and keep the monthly bill under twenty-five dollars. Use it *only* to connect with your kids when necessary, and in case of car emergencies. Used properly, a car phone can be an inexpensive insurance policy and a great safety device. It's a link to civilization if you run out of gas, get a flat tire, or find yourself in any sort of dangerous situation and need help.

And if you have a teenager who has just begun to drive, he can use the car phone to call you to let you know where he is and when he'll be home. No more excuses that he couldn't get to a phone.

Both you and your kids should know, however, that it can be dangerous to drive and talk on the phone at the same time. The *New England Journal of Medicine* recently reported that drivers using car phones are four times as likely to be involved in an accident as those who don't use car phones while driving. Teach your driving teenagers, by your own example, to pull off the road to make a call from a car or cellular phone.

If you have a business at home or use the phone a lot for computer work, it might be simpler for you to get a second line, which can be dedicated to a fax machine and computer modem. Carefully consider the expense and the actual convenience of equipment and services before you sign up for any more hookups.

All self-respecting businesses have business hours. If you work out of your home, let your callers know what those hours are and stick to them. People will call you around the clock if you let them.

It's so easy to let the phone take over our lives. Teach your kids how to use the phone (#33), establish convenient times for phone calls from other family members and associates, and don't let phone time eat into your time with your family.

27.

Learn about Computers, Software, and Cyberspace

WE'RE AN INFORMATION-ORIENTED CULTURE. Computers, software, and cyberspace connect us to that information. Besides being fun, efficient, and incredibly useful, computers are fabulous tools for creative activities such as writing and drawing, and for developing analytic skills involving math, science, and manipulation of large amounts of data.

Most kids have been using computers at school since the early grades. Vocabulary lessons, lab and book reports, current events assignments, and editing schoolwork are all much easier to do on a computer. Your child will be competing for grades with other kids who use computers. A paper with computer graphics, maps, and graphs will have a decided edge over a paper without these elements, no matter how diligently your child has worked on it.

By the time a child graduates from high school, she has to be completely computer literate in order to compete in today's job market. These days you put your child at a distinct disadvantage if you don't own a computer.

If you haven't already done so, here are some things to think about when selecting a basic computer system:

Decide whether you need a Macintosh or a PC.

If you have primary, elementary, or middle school children, call their computer teacher and find out what hardware they're using in school. Buy the same computer they're already using and don't look back. Most schools use Macintosh computers, making the decision a simple one. Macintosh by Apple is reliable, versatile, graphics-oriented, and user-friendly. Your kids will use their Macintosh happily for many years.

If you have older children, you might want to consider a PC-based computer that uses the Windows operating system. Young adults heading for college will probably be better served by transitioning to Windows while they're still in high school. This will give them an opportunity to get ready for the Windows environment they'll most likely face when they hit campus and, later, the business world.

When it comes to software, buying simple programs that make less demand on your computer's internal memory capacity is the better way to go, at least for kids. Keep in mind that annual upgrades are expensive, take up space on your hard drive, slow your computer down considerably, and usually aren't necessary if you've got a good basic program. Also, if you're not paying attention, it's possible to quickly spend on software—much of which is of questionable value—several times the money you've spent on the hardware.

You'll need a simple word-processing program so your children can write, and possibly a spreadsheet and graphing program so they can perform more complex art, math, and science projects. Again, consult with your kids' teachers. Whatever they're using at school is probably the easiest way to go. Also, most of the bundled software packages will be adequate for your kids, at least for starters.

If you have more than one child and only one computer, you'll need to set up a schedule so that each child gets time at the monitor.

It's difficult to keep track of what your kids are doing on the computer, and especially in cyberspace, if you're not computer literate yourself. I strongly urge you to get literate. Take a class, or ask someone—even a neighbor kid—to teach you the basics.

And keep an eye on your kids to make sure they're not accessing any compromising or inappropriate material on the Internet. Be sure to explain to them the dangers of communicating with strangers and divulging any private information, such as names, addresses, or phone numbers. One twelve-year-old daughter of a friend got into a chat room with a bunch of older boys. She went through a terrifying couple of days because they managed to convince her that she'd had sex on line and had lost her virginity.

If you keep the computer in a common area of the house, rather than in a bedroom, you can supervise your children's activities more closely.

If you suspect any wrongdoing, there are programs available that will access past activity or block inappropriate web sites.

Figure that once you've got a computer setup and the software to run it, the chances are good it will meet your kids' requirements for the next five years or longer before you'll need to buy anything else. Of course, there's nothing to say that you—and especially your kids—won't *want* to make changes. The temptation is strong to get the fastest, most powerful computer and as much software as your hard drive will hold, and then some. But, as with any other area of consumerism that can get quickly out of hand, try to keep your actual needs clearly in mind.

It costs from fifteen hundred to two thousand dollars for an adequate computer setup today. You might be able to spend a little less, and you can definitely spend a whole lot more, though with luck you may be able to acquire a used computer that will serve your kids' needs for a number of years.

Any way you look at it, computer systems and software are expensive. But a computer will be central to your children's careers and to their ultimate survival in tomorrow's world. If you have to, forgo the Walkman, video games, stereos, expensive CDs, and even (or most especially) the television in favor of a computer for your kids.

If you haven't already addressed the issue of computers, software, and cyberspace in your kids' lives, it probably won't simplify your life, in the short run, to have to think about it now. It will be even less simple, in the short run, to have to do something about it. But computers are a fact of life today, so it will certainly simplify your lives in the long run to do whatever it takes to make your kids computer literate.

If you set appropriate house rules (#11) for the computer, and monitor their use of it properly, it will be one of the most important investments you make in their future.

Five

THE INDEPENDENT CHILD

28.

Encourage Independence at an Early Age

WHEN A BABY leaves its mother's womb, it begins its journey toward an independence that is finally realized roughly eighteen years later, when the child leaves home. We have to help our kids make this transition from baby to toddler to child to confident young adult.

Your challenge is twofold. You have to prepare your child to handle life's situations as they arise. And you have to learn to recognize when your child is ready for new freedoms, and to graciously and willingly grant them.

Understand, and teach your kids, that some failure is inevitable. Treat any setback as a learning experience—for you and for them.

Watch for signs of readiness and respond to the signals you see and hear: a toddler waking up with a dry diaper is ready to be toilet trained; a child asking about letters is ready to learn the alphabet; kids watching carefully while you make dinner are ready to help in the kitchen.

But don't wait for your kids to ask for additional freedom. Parents often make the mistake of holding out until their children rebel before giving them a later bedtime, increasing their allowance, or permitting them to do things on their own.

Continually evaluate how much more freedom you can give your kids. Around the time of their birthdays discuss upping their allowance or giving them an extra half hour before lights-out. When they prove by good grades and responsible behavior that they can be trusted, give them even more freedom. During exam week last year, Peter asked to go to a Dave Matthews Band concert the night before an important chemistry exam. Vera and Tim said yes; he's maintained a good grade average and he'd studied for the exam the weekend before.

If your children see that you have confidence in their venturing farther and farther from the nest, if they see that you're glad when they assume greater responsibilities, and if they know you support their efforts toward self-sufficiency, they'll reward you with the same trust and respect you're offering them.

This is especially important when dealing with teenagers. Which is not to say you should allow your teens to be unsupervised. Quite the contrary. Teenagers need a different kind of supervision because drugs, alcohol, and sex have now become a serious factor in everyone's life. You've got to set curfews, insist they check in with you by phone at stated times, and make certain there's an adult present when they go to a friend's home, among many other things.

Let them know that if they abuse their freedoms, if their grades falter, or if they get involved with drugs, drinking, or other irresponsible behavior, their privileges will be revoked.

Being too liberal can be more harmful than being overprotective. Children need structure, security, and consistency in order to feel safe and know they're loved.

How do you know how much freedom your children can handle? Take a good, hard look at their behavior, their grades, their friends, and how well they comply with the rules you set. Peter has a perfect record in terms of being responsible about the freedom they give him, has a lot of common sense, and is realistic about his requests, so Vera and Tim generally let him do what he wants.

Some children are very literal and will follow your rules to the letter while bending the spirit of them as much as they can. Sasha was told by the school theatrical director that she couldn't bring food from home to a play rehearsal, so she and her friends ordered a pizza to be delivered to the school. ("But it didn't come from *home*, Mom.") The school officials were not amused.

Kids like Sasha, who have a gift for spotting loopholes, have to be watched a little more carefully, and should be rewarded with privileges only after they've demonstrated their ability to responsibly handle the freedoms they presently have.

One day that three-year-old clinging tenaciously to your leg will grow into a happy, independent young adult. It's not easy, of course. It takes lots of love, patience, guidance, wisdom, and a willingness on your part to allow your kids to make their own mistakes. But as your child gains independence, so do you, and your life becomes simpler.

29.

Try Some Other Separation Tactics

START YOUR CHILDREN on the road to independence by letting them know that it's okay if you're not always around. Enroll your three-year-old in a preschool; get baby-sitters to watch your kids at home. Let your children learn that by and large they can trust people other than Mom and Dad to look after their needs, and that they can be safe and even happy with other caregivers.

Start by leaving your child with a baby-sitter or at preschool or child care for just a short time while he gets used to a new situation. Gradually lengthen the time. Some kids don't mind longer separations, and others can't tolerate even short ones, so be sensitive to the individual needs of your children.

If they cry when you leave them but stop as soon as you're out of sight, you're okay. If they keep crying and then cling to you more than ever when you return, then you might wait awhile before venturing out again. Peter was always a very independent child. Sasha wanted only Vera or her Dad when she was little, but then got used to regular baby-sitters. Both were ready and happy to go to preschool when they were two.

Andrew, on the other hand, was a happy and independent baby who became very needy at two, and got terribly upset when Vera tried to take him to preschool. It wasn't worth the emotional struggle to get him to go, so she took him out of the program. Kids can benefit from the socialization skills they learn in preschool, but they have plenty of time to develop those skills as three- and four-year-olds. The following year, at three, Andrew was very content to go to nursery school.

Here are some more ways to ease separation anxiety:

1. Keep the number of separations in one day to a minimum. Don't come home between two errands and have to leave your child again. Organize your day or evening so you leave only once.
2. When your child is invited to a friend's, have the two kids go together directly from school to the friend's house. If your child comes home first, he may have a hard time leaving your side for the second time that day.
3. When you and your child go to a new place, hang around in the background until you see that he's comfortable in the new situation or until he's absorbed with an activity. Then say goodbye and leave.
4. Explain your other commitments. Let your children know that you have work to do, an appointment to keep, a doctor to see,

and that there'll be other situations where they simply can't go with you—either because you don't want them to or because there are places kids just can't go.

5. If your child has difficulty separating at bedtime, stay in a nearby room for a few minutes and sing or hum or make some kind of noise so he knows you're still there.

When children are little, give them opportunities to explore the outside world and see how interesting it is. Visits to the beach, the zoo, a museum, and other educational attractions (and, if possible, other towns and countries) inspire a lifelong curiosity to branch out to new places and learn about new things.

As your children get older, enroll them in summer day camp. And when they're older still, sleep-away camp provides a great opportunity for them to learn to fend for themselves.

Take advantage of overnight trips sponsored by local schools or churches. Peter took a weeklong historical tour with his high school class. It turned out to be a valuable education beyond the sites and museums they visited. It was his first experience as an independent young adult away from home, and it gave him a lot of confidence in his ability to depend on his own resources—which is, after all, one of our major goals for our children.

30.

Get Your Kids to Do as Much as They Can

THE MORE YOUR CHILDREN learn to do for themselves and for one another, the simpler your life becomes. From a very early age, without any prodding, kids are struggling to become more independent. Babies don't want to be held anymore—they want to crawl. Toddlers push their parents away in order to explore the world around them. Older children take on bigger challenges, until one day your sixteen-year-old is asking for the keys to the car.

Your children need to feel a sense of accomplishment in whatever task they've undertaken. Profusely praise their early efforts at brushing their teeth, getting dressed, pouring juice, frosting the cupcakes. Give them opportunities for independent successes. Let them climb the jungle gym without hovering, draw a picture without criticism, make a sandwich without carping about the mess they're making. The results of their efforts will be far from perfect, but they'll improve with time.

Don't make suggestions or interfere unless your kids ask for your help. If they get into a fix, try to ignore it, or offer help in the form of a delicately phrased question. "Can you get down from that branch by yourself?" is more constructive than "You're going to crack your head open! Don't move until I get a ladder!" "Remember to hold the glass while you're pouring" is better than grabbing the juice carton out of a child's unskilled hands and saying, "You're making a mess! I'll do it."

When Andrew started getting himself dressed, he decided that underwear was highly overrated considering the additional effort he needed to expend in order to get it on. Vera was just glad he'd finally taken the initiative to dress himself, and let him get comfortable with the essentials first before she insisted on underwear.

Obviously, you can't let your children do anything dangerous, but don't be afraid of the little bumps, bruises, and stumbles that are inevitable. Remember you won't always be there to protect and help them, so let them learn their limits under your supervision. Then you'll also be more confident about leaving them with someone else.

There are many things kids can do for themselves.

Toddlers can start to brush their teeth, comb their hair, climb in and out of the car seat, feed themselves with finger foods or with a spoon, and go up and down the stairs safely (turn them around backward at the top, and show them how to go down feetfirst).

Kids three to five years old can begin to dress themselves, open and close doors, get an apple out of the fridge, clear their plates from the dinner table, put their books and toys away, and wash themselves (with supervision) in the bath.

It's helpful to learn about the developmental stages a child goes through, especially when it's your first. I recently spoke to young parents who were frustrated that their thirteen-month-old wasn't yet able to feed himself with a spoon. He preferred—as all babies do at that age—to throw the spoon and his food on the floor. *Your Child: Birth to Age Five,* by Penelope Leach (Knopf, 1989), is a good primer for helping you recognize and understand these early stages.

Life becomes much simpler for you once your kids reach six or seven, by which time they should be fairly independent. They can get their own cereal, make a simple sandwich, pour a glass of juice, serve themselves at the dinner table, take care of their toys, be responsible for their personal hygiene, turn on the computer, and entertain themselves with a minimum of supervision.

After your kids reach seven you can begin to give them specific chores like emptying the trash or setting the table. Now they can begin to make a real contribution to your household. Don't let them use electrical or gas appliances without hands-on supervision until they're much older, but do encourage them to watch and help while you're cooking. And they can start to help their younger siblings learn to do things for themselves.

As they get older still, your children should take on more adult responsibilities. Peter mows the lawn, takes out the garbage, helps with heavy lifting, and shares the driving responsibilities. Sasha helps shop and put away groceries, and helps Andrew clean his room. All these things teach our kids to be self-reliant while simplifying our own lives—the best of both worlds.

31.

Teach Your Kids to Use the Appliances

"BUT I DON'T KNOW HOW IT WORKS." How many times have you heard that refrain when you've asked your children to start a load of laundry, turn on the dishwasher, or move the wet clothes from the washer to the dryer?

There's also the microwave, oven, mixer, blender, phone, answering machine, computer, radio, tape recorder, CD player, VCR, stereo—all things children need help with until they learn how to use them on their own.

Think about how much time you spend cooking, laundering, vacuuming, mowing, and toasting. Now think about how much time you could save if you taught your kids how to use your household appliances themselves.

So the next time your son asks, "Mom, did you wash my gym shorts yet? I need them tomorrow," simply escort him to the washing machine and show him how to use it.

And answer, "Dad, can I have an English muffin, and could you toast it, please?" with a toaster demonstration.

When more cereal falls on the floor than finds its way into the cereal bowl, pull out the broom and dustpan, and teach your child how to sweep it up.

Young kids of five and six can safely learn to turn on appliances that can't hurt them (and that they can't hurt): the TV, the VCR, and even the computer are all fairly benign—though they need to understand that stuffing cookies into the disc drive is not allowed.

By the time children are ten, they can use just about every household appliance by themselves except equipment that generates a lot of heat—they'll need supervision with stoves and ovens until they're about thirteen or fourteen. Sasha cooks a lot and knows how to use the oven and the range, but her parents make sure there's an adult around to see that everything remains under control.

When your kids are old enough to do major chores around the yard, make sure you teach them how to use the mower, leaf blower, lawn tractor, and other garden equipment safely. Closely supervise their initial adventures with any power tools. Vera and Tim have several acres of land, and Peter's been helping with the yard work since he was ten. He started out by hauling leaves in a cart hooked up to the tractor. Now he uses practically every piece of equipment they have, except for the chain saw—Vera prefers him in one piece.

32.

Show Your Kids How to Manage Their Own Space and Stuff

"MOM, WHERE ARE MY SHIN GUARDS? The soccer game starts in ten minutes!"

"Who took my library book? I left it on the kitchen table last night before I went to bed." ("You found it under my bed? How'd it get there?")

Think about how much time you'd save if you didn't have to stop what you're doing half a dozen times a day to hunt for your children's belongings. It will greatly simplify your life if you teach your kids to be responsible for their own things.

As with many areas of simplifying, the earlier you start, the easier it will be. When Peter was a baby, Vera and Tim were at his beck and call twenty-four hours a day. Amazed by this magical creature they'd brought into the world, they did everything for him: cleaned up his messes, picked up his toys, and bought him every little thing his heart desired.

Now, he's the only one of Vera's kids who doesn't put things back where they belong. He's never learned to return borrowed items, he lets candy wrappers lie where they fall, and Vera still has to remind him to wipe down the countertop after he's made himself a sandwich.

By the time Vera and Tim had figured out from sheer exhaustion that they'd overlooked an important part of Peter's education, it was too late. He was only four or five at the time, but the bad habits had been formed. They've spent ten years trying to break them, with some success, but the pattern runs deep. If you're indulging any of your children in the same way, you're not doing them or yourselves any favors.

Here are some steps you can take to help your kids form good habits right from the start:

1. Make sure all frequently used household items have a resting place and that your children know where things belong: the scissors go in the top desk drawer; the broom hangs on the hook in the utility room; the flashlight is kept in the kitchen cabinet; and so forth.

2. Teach your kids to put away whatever they use—their own stuff and yours. Getting this message across takes great patience in the beginning. But if you take the easy route and put it away for them, they'll never learn to do it themselves.

3. If your children don't clean up their messes after several reminders, take away television or other privileges until the job

is done. Or if your kids leave a pile of toys at the foot of the stairs, put the toys in a box and stow them away until the kids notice they're missing and agree to put them where they belong. Then be sure they do.

4. *Help* your kids clean up their rooms when they're little; don't do it for them.

5. Designate a place for their sports equipment, and make sure they stash gear there when they return from a game.

6. When your kids come in wet and muddy from a soccer game or Little League, teach them to carefully take the sodden mass of clothes straight to the washing machine—and when they're old enough, show them how to run the washer and dryer. No more mildewed sweatshirts or mud-encrusted jerseys in the back of a closet.

7. And teach your children that when they lose something, it's their responsibility to find it—not yours.

33.

Free Yourself from the Tyranny of the Phone

YOU'VE GOTTEN RID of all the extra phones and phone lines in the house; you're down to one line with several conveniently located extensions, plus an answering machine and possibly a car phone. You're saving lots of money on monthly phone bills, but it seems that you're still spending inordinate amounts of time on the phone organizing car pools, arranging play dates, and rescheduling doctor appointments.

Now is the time to start teaching your kids how to use the phone. By the time they're five or six, kids will want to answer the phone, and they might as well learn to do it properly. A simple "Hello" and "May I ask who's calling, please?" are easy to learn. Later on, getting them to take a fairly coherent message is not much more difficult.

Of course, it's simplest for kids to let the answering machine screen calls. They can pick up if it's for them, or if there is some pressing reason to speak to the caller. Otherwise, instruct them to let the caller leave a detailed message on the machine.

Teach your young child to say you're busy when you're otherwise indisposed, and to please call back. Kids have an uncanny way of blurting out exactly what it is you're doing and where you're doing it. This is more information than any caller needs to know.

As your children get older, get them into the habit of writing down whatever messages they take. Keep a pad and pencil next to the phone, so they'll know where to write the message and you'll know where to look.

Teach your children their own phone number, and how to dial 911 in case of an emergency.

Then they can begin to learn the phone numbers of their friends. With you standing by to advise them, your kids can arrange their own play dates. They must ask your permission before offering or accepting any invitations, and they have to consult with you on a good time for a visit, but that's all the input they need from you. If they need a ride somewhere, they can figure out who can give it to them and make the call.

Keep a list of all your children's friends' phone numbers by the phone for easy reference. Have your kids update it a couple of times a year.

Show your kids how to use the phone book and how to call Directory Assistance. They can call to get the local movie schedule or the new bus route. When soccer practice is postponed, they can call the next name on the telephone tree. You can teach them how to cancel a riding lesson, change a dentist appointment, order by mail, send flowers, call the hospital for patient information, and, eventually, even how to dial overseas. These are all things they need to know how to do eventually, so why not start them at an early age?

You can also teach them that they don't have to answer the phone just because it's ringing. Make it a practice never to answer the phone when you're having quiet time together, or when you're all just going out the door for an appointment. (You can give a quick listen to the answering machine to make sure the appointment you're going to isn't being canceled, then return the call when you won't be rushed, and when you won't be keeping other people waiting.)

If you've got kids who love to talk on the phone, establish a time limit for their conversations. Set a stove timer; when it goes off, they have to wrap up their call quickly and hang up. Insist that they do their homework and chores before they make any phone calls to friends.

Teach your kids to use the phone for quick one-on-one conversations and to save the socializing for after school and play dates. The phone is not for idle gossip, prank calls, hours-long discussions on who said what to whom, or conference call chains. Show your kids by example how to keep it simple—a friendly hello and short chat, then conduct your business and hang up.

34.

Help Your Child Become Financially Independent

WHEN YOUR CHILDREN become adults and find employment, they'll begin to receive regular paychecks. They'll have to know how to budget their money to pay for fixed expenses, and how to save money for an expensive item or a rainy day. When they're somewhere between the ages of six and eight it's time to start giving your kids an allowance so they can learn firsthand how to spend, budget, and save wisely.

How much do you give a child for an allowance? It depends to a large extent on the child, her level of maturity, her particular needs in terms of her school expenses and her mode of transportation to and from school, and your financial circumstances.

You may already have learned one of the basic truths about allowances. That is, after a while you forget how much your child is getting, and no matter how much you give them, the kids are constantly lobbying for a raise. So to help you remember, and to deflect harassment from the kids, one option might be to adopt the formula that Vera uses for her kids: She decided that from age seven or eight until age thirteen or fourteen, twice the child's age per month is an appropriate amount for the expenses her kids encounter.

So an eight-year-old would get sixteen dollars a month, with an increase to eighteen dollars when she turns nine. At ten it would be twenty dollars a month, and so on. The kids have to budget for any special items they want, along with their regular month-to-month expenses. The amount you decide on can be doled out weekly, biweekly, or monthly.

To encourage savings, you could offer to match whatever money your kids save each month. Make sure, though, that expenditures from savings are for parentally approved purposes.

Some parents require that a certain percentage of their kids' allowance be set aside for charity, though that requires extra enforcement on your part. If you believe in giving money to worthwhile causes, let your kids know when you're planning to make a donation to the arts or to an environmental cause, or a pledge to your church or synagogue, and give them an opportunity, or require them, to add some of their own money to the family contribution.

As a child gets older, his needs and his expenses change. Once Peter reached high school, Vera found it was much easier to figure out a fair amount that would take care of all his expenses for the year than it was to put up with his constant requests for more money. This amount is paid in twice-monthly increments, and Peter knows he can't ask for more money if he runs short at the end of his pay period.

Peter quickly learned, through trial and error, how to budget for clothes, shoes, school lunches, sports equipment, concert tickets, dates, savings, and entertainment. His folks still pay for his medical and educational outlays, such as the cost for a class trip. But now that he's driving, they deduct a portion of his allowance for their extra car insurance.

Not only has this system taught Peter how to handle money—he's much more careful about spending his own money than he ever was about spending theirs—it has also eliminated a lot of money hassles.

My parents established a similar system for me as I was growing up, and I'll always be grateful for the sense of confidence they gave me about handling my own money. They felt strongly—and most parents I talk to agree—that kids shouldn't be paid for doing routine household chores. Rather, regular chores—keeping their own room cleaned, taking care of their clothes, helping with dinner preparation and cleanup—are what children should be expected to do as members of the family.

But do consider paying your kids for special jobs. Baby-sitting for a younger child while you go grocery shopping is a freebie, but baby-sitting so you and your spouse can go out for dinner or a movie is a paid job. One-of-a-kind big jobs like painting, cleaning out the garage, washing the car, or spring yard cleanup are also good opportunities for your child to earn some extra money.

Six

SIMPLE PARENTING PRACTICES

35.

Develop a Close Relationship with Your Kids

CHILDREN WHO FEEL LOVED thrive physicially, emotionally, socially, and intellectually. Kids who are neglected, or who have never been closely connected with their parents, have difficulty forming relationships of their own, do poorly at school, defy authority, and tend to experiment with alcohol, drugs, and sex.

Here are some things you can do to help build a solid relationship that will survive the terrible twos, an emotionally charged adolescence, and all the years in between:

1. Tell your kids you love them. Never pass up an opportunity to tell your child you love him. It gets harder as he gets older and begins naturally to pull away, but continue to tell him you love him, and sneak in a kiss and a hug whenever you can. Don't get discouraged when he doesn't reciprocate. It's his job to establish his independence—and to appear not to want your affection—but it's your job to continue to be there for him, loving him all the while.

2. Show your kids you love them. Spend time with them every day, give them hugs and kisses, listen to their stories, play games with them. Go to their school conferences and concerts, cheer at their baseball games, and applaud their performances in school plays.

3. Accept your children for who they are. Much of our children's character is beyond our control. What we can control is how we deal with our kids and what we say. Encourage your kids' special interests and strengths. Don't try to make them into someone they aren't—your son may never be the baseball star you'd hoped to play catch with; your daughter may decide to play soccer instead of becoming the concert pianist of your dreams.

4. Love your children unconditionally. This means you love them no matter what. It doesn't mean you can't get upset with them; it just means you can't punish them by withholding your love when you're mad.

5. When you get angry with your child, address the issue, not his character. Even though he's done something wrong, that doesn't make him a bad person. Phrases that reinforce this idea are: "I love you very much, but I don't like what you've done," or "I'm disappointed in your behavior." Never say "What's wrong with you?" or "How can you be so stupid?" Communicate your displeasure, be firm about your rules, but never disparage his character.

6. Stay attuned to your child's problems and needs. As you continue the process of simplifying your life, keep in mind that one of the major reasons to keep life simple is so you'll be able to stay connected with your children. By doing so, you'll understand their normal ups and downs, so that when they have a problem you'll be able to see the change in their behavior and help them to deal with it.

For instance, if you have a four-year-old who's suddenly terrified of going to sleep, rather than force the issue and end up with a crying child and a tearful bedtime scene *take the time* to figure out a different approach. Maybe an incentive, such as an extra bedtime story or five more minutes of snuggling, will work for this child.

Or if you have a preteen who is suddenly sullen and uncommunicative, it may be a natural phase she's going through or she may be having problems socially or academically. You'll be able to intervene early because you know your daughter and you'll know when something's wrong. If you're attuned to your kids and the things that are happening in their lives, you'll know when to back off and when to press for explanations. Dr. Spock always said we *know* how to raise our kids. When we take the time, we can tap into our own intuitive knowledge and come up with workable solutions to our children's problems.

7. Find a mutual interest. As children grow up, they grow away from us as well. You can't force them to stay close, but you can find things to do together that will encourage a continued intimacy. This is especially important with teenagers—they'll become strangers if you don't find something you can do together.

   The earlier you establish the practice of doing things with your kids, the easier it will be to continue to be a part of their lives as they get older. And the more a part of your teenager's life you are—his drawing, riding, hiking, camping life—the more opportunities there are to talk about serious issues such as smoking, drinking, drugs, and sex.

8. Acknowledge their accomplishments. Tell your kids how proud you are of them. Let them know you notice their efforts, no matter how small—from dressing on their own, picking up their toys, or taking a phone message accurately, to improving their grades. Not only does this help to establish a bond between you and lets them know you're paying attention, but it gives them something to live up to.

36.

Keep Your Sense of Humor

LIFE CAN GET DIFFICULT. Juggling work and family, worrying about finances, dealing with children and aging parents, and keeping the house in a state of relative order and repair are only a few of the pressures that can weigh us down.

We greatly lighten our load when we learn to find the humor in our lives. And as much as we want to teach our kids to be serious and responsible, we don't want them to see adulthood as such a horrible burden that they decide they want to remain children forever.

Most issues with your children can be addressed with humor and goodwill. Make a game out of everyday tasks like doing chores, putting away toys, table manners, and other relatively mundane matters. Even when you're serious about getting a job done, inject some humor into the situation and it'll be a happier experience for all of you.

And if your kids do or say something funny even when they're "supposed" to be serious, don't forget to laugh. Laughing won't undermine your authority or sabotage the lessons your children are meant to be learning. Rather, they'll love you for your ability to appreciate the lighter side of life.

The other advantage to treating most problems lightheartedly is that when you *are* serious, your children will know you really mean business. They'll learn to hear it in your voice when you reserve your no-more-kidding tone for only the most significant issues, and they'll know they need to stop fooling around and mind what you have to say. Important issues include, among others, schoolwork, curfews, treating parents and other adults with respect, telling the truth, following through on promises, and fighting between siblings. And later, the profoundly serious issues include smoking, drinking, drugs, and sex.

Take time every day to have real fun with your kids. Be sure you're involved in an activity they love, like building with blocks, playing cards, working on a dollhouse, reading a story, playing tag or softball, windsurfing, or playing computer games.

Keep spontaneity in your lives. Every now and then break your normal routine: treat them to a hot fudge sundae, even it if spoils their dinner—or do it in place of dinner. Get everyone into the car and take them to a movie or to the park for a sunset walk along the river, just for the heck of it. Or offer, in exchange for a big hug and a kiss, to clear the table and do the dishes for them, just for tonight and just because you love them.

Strike a good balance between work and play, and be sure to do things that will give you and your children an opportunity to truly enjoy each other as people.

37.

Learn to Be Patient

THE KEY TO PATIENT parenting is accepting the fact that kids can't do everything as fast as or as well as you can, and learning to adapt your expectations to their abilities. Impatience and unrealistic expectations lead to constant battles, anger, and frustration—for you and for your kids.

Take walking, for example. Your legs are twice as long as your toddler's legs. Yet how often have you found yourself telling her to "hurry up" or "stop dawdling"? Instead, slow down and pace yourself to her speed.

How often do we say to our kids, "Hurry up and eat"? Kids can't eat fast, and shouldn't—it's not healthy to wolf down a meal. Yet we expect them to be able to eat as quickly as we do.

Getting themselves dressed, until they learn the knack, is an ordeal. They're too busy to change, can't find their favorite T-shirt, don't know the back of their underwear from the front, and struggle to get their socks and shoes on.

Toilet training, too, is a real challenge to one's patience—from dealing with accidents to looking for a bathroom at your local mall, especially when your daughter insisted she didn't have to go before you zipped her into her snowsuit.

As parents, our patience is constantly tested in one way or another: requests for glasses of water at bedtime; worries about monsters; much-needed sleep interrupted because of nightmares, illness, or bed–wetting; separation anxiety; mysteriously missing homework assignments; sibling rivalry with the accompanying pettiness, noise, and blame; the four-year-old who asks, "Why?" at nanosecond intervals, and the teenager who gets an A-plus in chemistry but can't remember to wipe the peanut butter off the countertop.

You simply have to take a deep breath, accept their behavior as a natural part of growing up, and adapt.

Schedule more time to get from one place to another.

Count on having to spend an extra five minutes waiting while your child looks for her lost toy or security blanket.

If you're tired, take a nap if you can—even a five- or ten-minute rest can make a difference in your state of mind. Or go to bed earlier.

Make a game of getting your child dressed. Use distraction as a tool when your patience has worn thin or you've gotten tired of a particular activity.

When the household gets too noisy, separate yourself from the chaos: either send the kids to their rooms, or go to your own room.

Whatever you do, don't get angry. Children don't have the ability or self-control to always do what you want them to as fast as you want them to do it. They're not misbehaving—it's just their natural slowness and immaturity.

When you do have a disciplinary problem, rather than blowing your top take the time to carefully consider your reaction. Or think about consequences for your child's behavior ahead of time so you'll be prepared with the appropriate response when you need it.

For instance, the next time your child refuses to help with a task, instead of yelling and threatening, calmly and patiently explain to her that she can't watch TV or play with any toys until the job is done. If she doesn't pitch in, take away that day's TV privileges or refuse the next request she makes of you, and explain why.

38.

Realize That It's More Than Just a Phase

CHILDREN MATURE in different ways and at different rates—infants become mobile; sweet babies turn into cantankerous two-year-olds; cuddly threes become independent but fearful fours. Each age brings its own peculiarities, and each child develops at his own pace—some are terrible threes instead of terrible twos, and others are never terrible at all.

With child-rearing books at hand and memories of your own childhood, you know that many of these stages will pass. But your children don't know this. For them, each moment is new; each experience is another challenge. And each challenge must be treated seriously.

Every stage of childhood is a building block kids use to construct the foundation for their future lives. With your help it can be a solid foundation of character, confidence, and hope. But if you say, "Oh, it's just a phase," that belittles the importance of what's going on with them at that particular time. Kids can get stuck at any point in their development if they don't get the help and understanding they need. That's one reason there are teenagers who can't do anything for themselves and still throw tantrums to get what they want.

Parents who dismiss their kids' experiences as "just a phase" overlook the seriousness and depth of their kids' feelings and do them a great disservice. That's when kids start to think their parents don't understand, aren't listening, or simply don't care, and turn to their friends for validation. And then it's out of your hands altogether. Here are some ways to get through difficult times:

1. *Carefully examine the problem.*
   If your child is preverbal, find out what triggers a tantrum, bedtime difficulties, or aggressive or otherwise unwanted behavior. Kids often throw tantrums when they're tired, so try moving their nap or bedtime up. Bedtime and aggression problems are often caused by too much television, so keep the TV off the child's routine for a few days and see if things improve.

   Use the same approach for other problems—figure out the cause, and fix it. Just make sure you try only one solution at a time and evaluate its effect. That way, you'll have a better idea of what works than if you change several things at once.

   If your child is older, carefully observe what triggers problem behavior. Maybe your son talks back after playing with a certain friend, or your daughter becomes fearful after being left with a particular baby-sitter. Watch them carefully, and then talk to them about what's going on.

2. *Listen to your children.*
Carefully listen to what your kids say without being judgmental or critical. Sometimes they know exactly what's wrong, but they don't want to tell you because they're afraid of your reaction. Avoid being defensive, derisive, sarcastic, or hysterical when a child starts to tell you what's going on. Rather, be rational, reasonable, and open to whatever they have to say. Look at the situation from their point of view, and help them come up with an answer or a solution that will meet *their* needs.

And sometimes they don't know what's wrong. Then you have to listen even more carefully, put together the clues, and sort out what's going on.

3. *Don't be part of the problem.*
Maybe you're exacerbating the situation despite your best intentions. Are your restrictions so prohibitively severe that a child struggling for independence feels smothered? Are you so busy working that your kids think you don't care about them anymore? When they try to talk to you, do you put everything aside and really listen? Help them solve the problem rather than contributing to it.

4. *Correct inappropriate behavior.*

If your child is doing something wrong, you have to assert your authority firmly and remind him of the consequences if his behavior continues. A bad "phase" drags out longer when a parent is inattentive to a child's needs, is inconsistent in dealing with a specific problem, or is overly concerned with pleasing the child.

5. *Ask what you can do to help.*

Sometimes a child is simply overwhelmed with growing up. Let your child know you're there for him and that you understand. Ask if there's anything he'd like you to do to help him through an especially hard time. Just knowing you support him if he needs you will help.

And if he does need something from you, make sure you do your best to provide it.

Let the fact that your child is growing up comfort you when one particular time seems overwhelmingly difficult—toddlers and teens are the hardest for most parents. With proper patience and guidance from you, your kids will one day launch confidently into adulthood, and you'll have forged a friendship with them based on successfully working through all the tender and tumultuous stages of their young lives.

39.

Tell the Truth and Expect the Truth

IN ORDER TO HAVE A GOOD RELATIONSHIP with your children you have to be able to trust them to tell the truth. Start by setting a good example—they must see that you keep your promises and never lie to them, not even little white lies. Show your children you trust them. They'll be less likely to break that trust if they know you believe in them.

But sometimes they will lie. How will you know? And what can you do?

Kids lie because they don't want to get into trouble. This is a very powerful motivation—stronger, and easier for a child to understand, than the underlying principle of telling the truth. A lesson they need to be reminded of time and again is that lying will get them into more trouble than telling the truth will. ("I don't care that you broke the vase; accidents happen. But I do care that you lied about it.")

Once you have the evidence that a bold-faced lie has been told, you must confront your child with the facts. Never ask him if he's the offender or if he's lying—he'll almost always deny it. Simply state the truth as you know it: "Robert, there were three dollars on the counter when I went upstairs with the laundry, and now they're missing. You're the only one home. I know you took them; now please give them back."

Most kids will confess when exposed, but others will cross their hearts and swear it wasn't them. Explain again why you're certain of his guilt, and give him a time-out (#42) until he comes clean.

If he still won't confess, remind him of the importance of telling the truth and the irrefutable evidence you have of his guilt—and consider the affair closed. There's no point in both of you digging in and getting nowhere. You know what happened and your child knows you know and has been disciplined—that's the best you can hope for in a situation like this.

You can take this approach only if you have an airtight case or a reliable eyewitness. What do you do if you're just suspicious? If you try to investigate by asking direct questions like, "Did you break the cookie jar?" you'll get only indignant denials. You can ask an impartial third party who may have witnessed the event.

Or you can try confronting the child as though you have evidence of his wrongdoing. A guilty child usually won't argue—he thinks you know more than you do—while an innocent child will be genuinely confused, frustrated, and resentful of the false accusation. So be prepared to apologize if you've confronted the wrong child.

If you still can't get a straight answer, give up. Better to presume innocence than punish a child for something he may not have done.

When you do catch your child in a lie, calmly explain to him how serious it is and how difficult it is to reestablish trust once it's been broken. Be extra vigilant about his behavior—you have every reason to suspect he may lie again.

Honesty becomes especially important when your kids become teenagers. You have to be able to trust them before you can let them take on the responsibilities of driving the family car or going on trips away from home.

40.

Keep the Lines of Communication Open

YOUNG CHILDREN love to tell you about the teensiest details of their lives. They share their experiences, tell fantastic stories, and ask endless questions. It's fun to be such an integral part of their lives. But as they get older, around twelve, they become much more reluctant about sharing, if not downright uncommunicative. Conversations turn into parental monologues. Teenagers in particular may respond with either an occasional "okay" or just a grunt.

In order to give your children the guidance they need, you must know what's going on in their lives: who their friends are, what they do together, what they're learning in school, how they get along with their teachers, what their interests are, what their problems are, and all the other elements that make up the daily minutiae of their lives.

One way to get a reticent child to talk is by asking very specific questions. How often have you asked your child, "What did you do in school today?" only to get a curt "Nothin'," for an answer? You've got to be more specific: "Who did you play with at recess today?" or, "What are you doing in art class now?" are the types of questions that will open a dialogue. Then follow up with more specific questions. "And what did Jennifer paint?" "Did you like the painting that Jason did?"

Start early on with your kids to get them *into the habit* of talking with you about their day and their feelings about what happened. Naturally there'll be times a child won't want to talk about something. Don't press the issue; but be sensitive to what's going on, and available when she does decide to open up.

Mealtime or when you're in the car and have a captive audience are good times to share the events of the day with each other. And bedtime is a great time for a snuggly chat with a younger child or a quiet conversation with an older one.

This is one good reason to minimize the use of Walkmans, TVs, stereos, and computers—or at least to set specific rules about when they can be used. They're such a convenient way for kids to close off from their parents, their siblings, or anyone else.

Again, when you converse with your children try not to judge or be critical about anything they tell you. It's not necessary to make a lesson out of every experience your child shares with you. If you're disturbed by something, by all means discuss it with your child, but refrain from lecturing, arguing, name-calling, shouting, or any other surefire conversation stoppers.

There are many times when simply acknowledging what your child is feeling is a better approach than trying to give advice:

"You're feeling angry" (or hurt or embarrassed or whatever) will let a child know you're really paying attention. That may be all the assurance she needs to open up and talk about it.

When she does, be sure to give her your full attention. Set your work aside, turn off the television, or stop whatever it is you're doing and simply be there with her.

Often, if she can talk about it, she can come up with her own solutions and won't need your advice. Whenever appropriate, ask questions like "So what would you like to do about this?" or "How do you think this should be handled?" to get her thinking about her own solutions.

Establish the *expectation* early on that you and your child can talk about what's going on in her life. Show by your interest and your involvement that you each have a responsibility, as members of the family, to keep the lines of communication open. If you're still having problems, read *How to Talk So Kids Will Listen and Listen So Kids Will Talk,* by Adele Faber and Elaine Mazlish (Avon, 1991).

Seven

SIMPLE DISCIPLINE
STRATEGIES

41.

Come Up with Logical Consequences

DISCIPLINE AND GUIDANCE are positive actions that demonstrate respect for the integrity of a child. Discipline is based on love and logical consequences and teaches self-control.

Punishment is a negative force that erodes a child's feelings of self-worth. It is based on power and fear, and it creates distance between you and your child.

You don't want your relationship with your kids to be based on fear. They need to feel that parents are a safe haven in an otherwise unpredictable world. Fear teaches them to be good because if they aren't they'll be punished, not because it's the right thing to do. As a result, many kids will wait until their parents are not around to misbehave.

The purpose of discipline is to teach children how to behave, and to help them develop a good conscience so they can learn right from wrong. Even though they may test you from time to time, they need your discipline in order to feel safe and secure. You need to be consistent and firm, especially when your kids are testing limits. But you also need to be loving and patient when your kids make mistakes.

And kids never stop making mistakes—they make old ones, new ones, messy ones, dangerous ones, funny ones, and hurtful ones. These experiences are their education. They have to learn that it's natural to make mistakes, but there are consequences to be paid. The concept of logical consequences means that their actions and your response need to be related. Don't get mad. Rather, calmly state the problem and make your child part of the solution.

Here's a list of common problems and their logical consequences:

Problem: Kids are fighting over a toy.
Solution: Calmly but resolutely take the toy away from them. Return it after exacting a promise from both that they'll share nicely. Don't try to figure out who had it first unless you've actually witnessed the event, in which case, return it to the wronged child.

Problem: A child knocks over a glass of milk.
Solution: Cleaning up is the child's responsibility—help only as much as you need to.

Problem: Your child hits or hurts another child.
Solution: One warning, then, if it happens at a friend's house, take your child home. If it's at home, a time-out (#42) would be appro-

priate. Tell your child there will be no more play dates for a few days and this usually corrects the problem.

Problem: Your child breaks television or telephone rules.
Solution: Suspend TV or phone privileges for a day or two.

Problem: Broken curfew.
Solution: Set and enforce an earlier curfew for a while.

Kids will repeat behavior patterns until they're stopped. It may seem easier to be lenient "just this once," but children don't understand leniency—they just see that you're not serious about your rules. There'll be a "next time" until you've finally had enough and put a stop to it.

Discipline your child on the spot. The first infraction is met with a warning, the second with consequences. If your kids know you mean what you say, they'll respect your authority. Pushover parents get mercilessly trampled by their unruly children, who go on to wreak havoc on the world at large.

Logical consequences don't mean dire ones. Grounding a child or taking away privileges for too long a period doesn't usually help. Kids, especially teenagers, will just get angry, belligerent, or withdrawn if the consequences are unreasonably severe. The objective is to nudge them back on track, not bulldoze them into submission.

42.

Use Time-outs

PUTTING A CHILD in time-out is another useful tool for your disciplinary arsenal. Making a mess or breaking a curfew has obvious logical consequences, but some infractions don't. Hitting a sibling, stomping around the house in a foul mood, throwing a tantrum at home, and talking back to a parent are all examples of inappropriate behavior for which it's difficult to create a consequence. In these instances the best approach is to put your child in time-out.

Time-out means that you separate your child from the family, from whoever he's picking on or annoying, and from anything he's doing that's fun. And he has to stay apart for a set amount of time, or until he decides that he's going to change his behavior. Don't engage your child in conversation during a time-out. If he tries to leave before his time is up, separate him again and add another minute to the time-out.

There are two levels of severity for a time-out. In the gentler time-out, the parent sends the child to his room. If your child has the array of toys and games many kids have in their rooms, this might seem as though you're sending him to Toys R Us for misbehaving. But often what you really need is a break from each other, and sending him to his room fulfills that need.

If you want to make more of a statement with your time-out, put him somewhere boring, like the bottom step of the staircase, or on a chair at a vacant dining room table. Whatever you choose, be prepared to police the time-out, and remember to tell your child when his time-out is up. Setting a kitchen timer for the appropriate amount of time helps.

Time-out works for several reasons. First, it gives everyone time to cool off and to think about the issue at hand. Second, children don't like to be removed from the action—especially if they have to spend ten interminable minutes staring at a blank wall while the rest of the family are free to do whatever they want.

Most experts suggest that a time-out should last as many minutes as the child is old in years, so a two-year-old would have a two-minute time out, a three-year-old three minutes, and so on. Don't go overboard by assigning an hours-long time-out—you want to correct your child's behavior, not banish him.

Of course, there'll be times when your child will test you by repeating the inappropriate behavior each time he rejoins the family. In this case, keep adding minutes to the time-out until he's ready to behave himself.

It's possible, too, because time-outs are so easy, to overuse this technique. Consider trying a different course of action, such as using logical consequences (#41). Try to understand why he's being so stubborn. Is he hungry or tired? Are you spending enough one-on-one time with him? Is he having trouble at school? Solve the underlying problem and you'll correct the behavioral one.

One mother, who is also a schoolteacher, told me she uses time-outs in the classroom if she feels angry or out of control, as a way to remove herself from a potentially explosive situation. This sets a good example for her students, too, because they then learn to use the time-out to identify their own emotions. And identifying them is the first step toward managing them.

Encourage your child to use his time-out to think about his behavior and how he might do things differently next time he's in a similar situation.

43.

Be Consistent

I RECEIVED A HEARTENING LETTER from a mother who successfully raised four kids as a single parent with no help, financial or otherwise, from her former husband. And though it meant some lean years, she put herself through college, too, so she'd be better able to support them.

Her secret? To simplicity and organization, she added *consistency*. Her kids knew what to expect. She didn't get upset over something one day and overlook it the next. They abided by rules that remained constant over time. They respected her because she was always available to them when they needed her, and because she showed a sincere and consistent interest in their thoughts and feelings.

Children require structure. They need a solid foundation from which they can explore the world, and a place that feels safe when things out there seem scary.

This sense of security comes from consistency. If kids aren't wary of the mood you're in, they can confide in you. If they know you won't yell, they can confess their mistakes. If they know you'll sympathize, they'll cry on your shoulder. If they know you'll listen, they'll tell you about their hopes and dreams (and maybe even tell you what they did in school today).

If they know you expect it, they'll help with the chores, refrain to a great degree from fighting with each other, and adopt the manners you've taught them.

But parents have to be consistent no matter what mood their children are in. Kids have a knack for taking advantage of loving, caring parents. "You're so mean," "I hate you," and, the worst, "I wish you were dead" cut to the core of your being.

You have to be consistent in the face of this kind of anger. It will pass. If you know you've been reasonable and the rules you've set are appropriate, then remain calm but firm, and wait out the storm. Your children must see that you won't be manipulated.

Whether you're an authoritative parent or a more permissive one, being consistent works because it creates a secure, predictable world for your children.

44.

Teach Your Kids to
Take Responsibility for Their Actions

KIDS DON'T LIKE to get into trouble. In truth, nobody likes it much. The natural response to getting caught is to try to find someone to blame:

"He hit me first!"
"She made me do it!"

Or to feign ignorance:

"I didn't know my project was due today."
"I don't know how."

Making excuses can easily become a habit. Children need the good example of their parents to learn how to be responsible for their own behavior. And you have to insist that your kids admit to the part they play in their own troubles.

There'll be exceptions, such as when the dog really does eat the homework, but they're rare. Your kids must take responsibility for their actions, their choices, and ultimately for their lives. How do you teach them to do these things?

Set a good example. Don't blame *your* parents for your problems, the economy for your debts, bad teachers for your children's shaky academic performance, your spouse for your unhappiness, or an insensitive boss for your stalled career.

When we accept responsibility, we can change things for the better. When we blame others for our failings, we become the victim. Teach your kids that having people's respect is preferable to having their pity—and that you never gain respect by whining and pointing your finger at someone else.

Allow your children to see that mistakes are inevitable and that the best course of action is to accept them, learn from them, and move on. Let them hear you say, "I really blew it this time," and, "I'm sorry; I won't let it happen again." and, most importantly, "How can I do things differently next time?" Then when your kids make mistakes, admitting it won't seem like such an unimaginably horrible thing. They'll be more willing to admit they're wrong and apologize or correct the situation.

The twelve-year-old son of a friend of mine was caught cheating on a test. First he tried to blame the teacher for making the material too difficult. Then he admitted that he'd cheated, but only on one question—which was supposed to make the situation better.

Fortunately, his mother would have none of it. She had her son write the teacher a note explaining that he understood his mistake and was sorry he had cheated. The letter reestablished a relationship of trust between the teacher and the student. Instead of making a bad situation worse with denials and accusations, the incident was acknowledged and soon forgotten.

Don't cover up for your kids. Too many parents want to protect their children from unhappy consequences. Vera's kids have asked her to write notes excusing them from homework they didn't finish on time. They've asked her to drive ten miles to school with a homework assignment that was left by mistake on the kitchen counter. At first, she felt sorry for them and helped out, but they began to rely on her as a backup. They got lazier instead of getting better.

Finally, she realized she was going to have to let them face the consequences. When she stopped rescuing them and refused to deliver their lunches and assignments, they became much more organized and responsible.

Kids also have to learn that in addition to being responsible for their things, they have to be responsible for their personal relationships and for people's feelings. They have a responsibility to their friends, family, teachers, acquaintances, and to the community. They need to recognize that it's within their power to either strengthen these relationships or undermine them.

45.

Pick Your Battles

WHEN MY FRIEND Liz was a contentious teenager, her mother would get just as mad at her if she left her bed unmade as she did when Liz was two hours late for her curfew. Her mother's reaction to all of her infractions, large or small, was the same—she'd yell, lecture, and send Liz to her room.

Liz's friends used to watch bewildered as she, knowing her mother was going to be mad anyway, did lots of things she wasn't supposed to do in order to get them all under what she called "the same mad."

Liz didn't learn until much later in life about the difference between large and small transgressions. And it took her many years to understand that in the real world she'd ultimately be held responsible for what she did wrong. Fortunately for her children, Liz made the decision early on to be more discriminating in picking her battles with her own kids.

Most disciplinary problems you encounter can be solved by imposing logical consequences. Remember the scales of justice, and don't overreact in the heat of a battle. If you feel you're going to blow up and say things you'll be sorry for later on, force yourself to count to ten while you compose yourself before addressing the problem. It's all right to tell your kids you need time to consider your options.

As we've seen, the easiest problems have obvious consequences—clean a messy room, put your tennis gear where it belongs, and the like. For more difficult problems—bad grades and sibling rivalry—there are other approaches you can take (#57).

And then there are the huge problems like lying, stealing, drug and alcohol abuse, and sexual misbehavior. These are the battles. Your children must understand that these issues are vitally important to you, and why. Discuss the dangers of these behaviors, and let your kids know you're fully committed to dealing with them seriously. Don't leave any question in their minds as to how you'll react.

Get clear in your own mind about which areas are most important to you, and pick your battles carefully. Don't squander your big guns on petty wrongdoing. Don't go ballistic when your child breaks a dish or eats candy before dinner. If you find your child sneaking a cookie, it's not the same as stealing from your wallet. Experimenting with hair color is not the same as experimenting with drugs.

Keep your perspective, and base your reaction on the degree of your child's disobedience. If you train yourself to make your reaction appropriate to the deed, your kids will understand that some things are more serious than others. This will be especially important for them to know once they hit their teens.

46.

Praise and Correct in Specific Terms

"Annie, what a great picture you've made! What is it?"

WHAT'S WRONG with this reaction to a child's drawing? You're obviously interested, and it sounds encouraging to your ears. But this kind of praise can actually backfire on you.

The child's obvious response is, "If it's such a great picture, how come you don't know what it is?" Children will notice contradictions like this and be quick to question the sincerity of your compliment.

It's much better to say, "Annie, why don't you tell me about your picture?" This way, your child can describe the drawing without feeling somehow inadequate or getting indignant.

Generalized praise like "great picture" isn't as meaningful to children as finding something specific about their performance or behavior. "I like the bright colors you used in your picture" is more effective than "great picture." And "I'm very proud of you; you've brought your science grade up from a B to a B+" is better than "Good report card."

Specific praise shows that you're really interested and paying attention. Make an effort to avoid dismissive comments. Saying, "That's nice, dear," without looking at what your child is trying to show you erodes her self-esteem. Specific praise gives her confidence in your interest and lets her know you really care.

Corrections work the same way, and should always be framed as suggestions. You have to be more sensitive about criticizing your children than about praising them, because thoughtless criticism can do real, long-term harm, whereas thoughtless praise is still praise.

Corrections, therefore, should be gently delivered, not insensitively blurted out, and should never be used to humiliate a child. Tell your child first what she did right, and praise her for it, and then, if appropriate, offer your suggestion on how she might improve. Sometimes it's better to simply offer your praise and hold your tongue regarding improvements.

Give your kids encouragement when they attempt something new and it doesn't work out quite right the first few times. Don't say, "You've put the fork on the wrong side of the plate." Instead, say, "Thanks for being such a big help. The next time could you please put the fork on the left?"

If your child has drawn a picture of her dad without hands or minus his nose, ask how he's able to drink his coffee or smell the roses instead of bluntly remarking, "He doesn't have hands," or "Where's his nose?" It seems like such a small thing, but it means a lot to a child.

When your five-year-old son bops his little sister over the head with his baseball bat, don't call him a "bad boy." That's not the message you want to send. Instead say, "I know you're a good boy, but hitting your sister is not accepable behavior in this household. Time-out until you can play nicely together."

Address the behavior, not the child. You want to prevent a repeat performance of the assault and teach the kids to play well together, not make your children think they're bad. Calling a child bad doesn't leave any room for redemption and gives little encouragement for improvement. A child thinks: I must be bad if they called me bad. Bad kids do bad things; and, What's the use of doing anything good if they're convinced I'm bad?

Kids will live up to the labels you assign them, good or bad. "She's the artist in the family," discourages other siblings from trying their hand with drawing or painting, and may keep the artist from taking up sports or playing a musical instrument.

The same can be said of labels such as shy, outgoing, athletic, hyper, funny, smart, and so on. Kids inevitably change, and labels only hold them back.

Remember that no amount of criticism evokes love; love evokes love. Be explicit and loving in your praise and corrections. Encourage your children's specific abilities while treating them as individuals capable of great accomplishments in many areas. Your kids will then have an opportunity to grow without being burdened by labels or limited by someone else's notion of who they are.

47.

Treat Your Kids with Respect

HOW YOU TREAT YOUR CHILDREN sets the example for how your children will treat you, their own children, and other people throughout their lives. Kids echo the words they hear and mimic the behavior they see. You probably were taken aback when you first heard yourself in your child's words (or heard your mother in yours!).

How do you show children respect and still maintain your authority?

1. Speak calmly instead of yelling. Yelling is demeaning and only helps to escalate a conflict and detract from the original issue.
2. Be firm, not mean.
3. Reassure kids when they're scared, rather than dismissing their fears.
4. Be as polite to your children as you want them to be to you.
5. Deal thoughtfully with inappropriate behavior instead of being harshly critical.

6. Assume you can learn as much from your kids as they can learn from you.

7. Correct your children's behavior in private. Doing so in public is humiliating.

8. Respect your child's wishes and choices, unless they're inappropriate, dangerous, or hurtful.

9. Trust your kids to do the right thing.

10. Don't tell potentially embarrassing stories about things your kids have done, especially in front of them and without their permission.

11. When you're with other adults—your friends, parents of your children's friends, the clerk at the checkout counter— acknowledge your child's presence and listen to and comment on any contribution she may want to make to the conversation. Let her know by your reaction that you value her opinions and that you appreciate her willingness to participate.

Children are people too—just because they're shorter doesn't mean their feelings are any smaller than ours. If your kids know you respect them, they'll be far more likely to respect you in return.

48.

Learn the Art of Making a Deal

WE WANT OUR CHILDREN to behave well because it's the right thing to do. The reality, however, is that most young children are extremely self-centered and do things because it's in their own best interest. Until the age of five or six, they basically just want what they want because they want it, and they want it right this minute.

Then things begin to improve, and you start to see signs of conscience, compassion, and self-control in your young companions. From the time they're six or seven until they're eleven or twelve, kids tend to be relatively sweet and compliant. Gentle reminders that it's bedtime are enough to hurry them upstairs; a request for help is usually quickly accommodated.

And then they hit adolescence.

Once again, as when your kids were much younger, the sun rises and sets over their own wants and needs. As much as you'd like to hope that by now your young adults will know how to behave appropriately and selflessly, this is the time when they'll test their limits and yours. Their desires will be the driving force behind their behavior. The selfish child is back, but more clever and much bigger.

You want your kids to listen to you, respect your rules, and happily do their chores and homework, but there'll be times when they'll procrastinate. They'll argue until the bitter end to get out of their obligations. Some kids are worse than others, and some ages are more combative than others. That's when you need to make it worth their while to do your bidding. That's when you need to make a deal.

"Sure, you can watch the Discovery channel—when your homework is done."

"Mow the lawn, and then I'll drive you into town."

"Get your grades up, and then we'll talk about a car."

You want to employ simple, straightforward deals that the youngest child can understand. Deal making is much more successful, and less draining, than arguing, cajoling, and threatening.

Don't confuse making a deal with bribery. Bribery is an "if . . . then," all-or-nothing proposition, usually with an unrelated reward attached to desired behavior: "If you stop bugging me, I'll get you a candy." Bribery backfires because children realize that next time they can get candy the same way. Never reward bad behavior with a treat.

A deal is a logical pact. The child gets what he wants after he fulfills his responsibilities. "Help me with the groceries and you can pick something out for yourself." This is not to say your child should be rewarded every time he helps out, but teach your children that their obligations come first, and that their desires will be respected if they pitch in and do their part.

49.

Teach Good Manners

GOOD MANNERS are the backbone of a civilized society. They make our encounters with people more pleasant and our daily struggles more tolerable. They create a strong first impression, and they pave the way to good jobs, smooth relations with family and friends, and an easier time out in the real world.

You can start teaching your children manners as soon as they can say "Please." Make sure they've learned all the basics before adolescence swings into high gear—you don't want self-absorbed and moody teenagers who are rude as well. This can make an already difficult stage unbearable.

Set an example for your kids with your own good manners. And don't make a distinction between how family members are treated and how one treats the rest of the world. Hostile and rude behavior is unacceptable anywhere, under any circumstances.

Children will sometimes forget their manners, as we all do when we're frustrated, tired, or angry. If you start with high expectations and your kids are basically polite, these lapses will result in still tolerable behavior. But children who have been held to lower standards will become insufferable.

Here are some basic manners you might want to consider:

General

1. Saying "Please" and "Thank you" should be as automatic as breathing. Insist that your kids use a proper tone of voice when they make a request; don't allow them to whine, ever.
2. When your kids bump into someone, they should say "Excuse me," or "I'm sorry."
3. Teach your children to apologize when they've done something wrong. ("What do you say to Matthew?" gives greater freedom for sincere expression than the rote "Tell Matthew you're sorry.")
4. Your kids should open doors for and offer their chairs to their elders.
5. When your kids receive a gift, teach them to write a thank-you note. One reader shared her family policy on this issue: If the notes don't get written, the gifts get returned. She pointed out that because her kids know she'll follow through on any of her policies, they got into the habit of sending thank-you notes, so she's never had to send anything back.
6. This goes against the grain of traditional etiquette, but these days a phone call is also a simple and appropriate way to express

ifts sent by mail—and it gives the kids an opportu-
o faraway friends and relatives at the same time.
rd from another reader who has her child send his
thank-you notes by E-mail to those friends who have a computer.

Introductions

1. Teach your kids how to make a proper introduction: A citizen is always introduced to the queen, the student to the teacher, a young friend to the grandparent, and so on. For example, "Mom, I'd like you to meet my friend Laura."

2. Children should stand when meeting or greeting an adult.

3. Teach your kids to introduce themselves. They can start with their friends' parents. Have you ever had a youngster turn up at the front door and not had a clue who they are? "Hi, you must be Hannah's mom. I'm Maria," would be a refreshing icebreaker.

4. A handshake is proper upon introduction. Kissing is generally for relatives and close friends, and it's all right if your children don't want to be kissed. That's their prerogative. Try to get them to politely avoid the kiss rather than to grimace or say, "Yuck."

5. "It's a pleasure to meet you," is very impressive coming from a child, but consider it a miracle if you ever actually hear it. You can teach it anyway.

6. Eye contact should be maintained throughout an introduction.

Visits

1. Your kids may decline an invitation with a simple "No, thank you."
2. When they accept an invitation, they must attend the event— barring illness or a family emergency.
3. At the end of your child's visit, he should make a special point of thanking his friend's parents.

Conversation

1. Don't interrupt when someone else is speaking.
2. Turn the TV off during a conversation.
3. "What?" or "Huh?" are unacceptable forms of the much more polite "Excuse me?" "Pardon me?" or the casual "What did you say?"
4. Don't allow swearing.
5. Don't allow your kids to say "Shut up" to anyone.

Teaching manners to kids is seldom easy, though many common courtesies can be taught by simple example. Your kids will no doubt need to be gently reminded about manners on a daily basis. This is not something you can expect them to learn and remember right away, so be patient and stay calm. But remember, it's much simpler to establish good manners than it is to break bad ones. And when they have good manners, your kids are much more enjoyable to be around.

50.

Never Forget That You're the Parent

KEEP IN MIND that one of the greatest advantages you have when it comes to dealing with disciplinary issues is that you're the parent. While parenting comes with many responsibilities, it also gives you certain rights—and powers. Properly and lovingly wielded, parental power can be your greatest ally.

You're bigger, older, wiser, more experienced, have better judgment, and are more capable of seeing the big picture than your kids. You run the house, make the rules, set the standards for behavior, and are in the position to discipline inappropriate behavior. The sooner you teach your kids to honor your position as parent, the easier it will be to fulfill your job of raising them.

This is not to say that you'll always be right, or that there won't be times when your kids will have a better answer than you do. But in the final analysis, you *are* the parent. There'll be many times when that is reason enough for you to make the final decision about how a situation will be handled and to simply overrule the objections they may throw in your way.

And sometimes it's absolutely essential that you do that. How many times have you seen a parent give up on a child, or give in to a tantrum because he doesn't know what to do. Usually when this happens that parent has forgotten—either for the moment, or permanently—that he is the parent, and that it's up to him to see that his child abides by his decision, even if it's only until he can make a better one. And most of the things we've talked about in this chapter, such as imposing logical consequences, using time-outs, and learning the art of making a deal will help you do that.

Obviously this is not a license for you to be a tyrant, ruling through manipulation and punishment. Nor should you dictate your child's every behavior. Not only is that extremely detrimental to kids, but parents who do this take away their children's initiative and voice, and leave them unable to express themselves, explore the world, or learn to be autonomous and independent young people.

Then there are parents who want to be their children's best pals. They're afraid of disciplining or setting rules because they don't want to offend their kids or do anything that would make their kids upset with them. They're so concerned with having their children like them that they forget to be parents. And the kids often suffer because of it. You can listen to your children without relinquishing your role as the decision maker.

Children need their parents to provide love, structure, rules, guidelines, and discipline more than they need their friendship.

Kids who live without structure can develop behavior problems. They expect the world to revolve around them and their needs, and they grow up oblivious to the needs of others.

Frequent tantrums, whining, a disregard for rules, inappropriate or aggressive behavior, constant demands, and an inability to share are some of the signs that your child needs more structure—needs you to be the parent. Some children sadly conclude that their parents don't love them if they don't care enough to figure out how to parent them.

If you establish your authority as the parent, and lovingly maintain that authority through your children's early years, you'll have created kids who respect you for who you are as well as for being their parent, and loving friendships will follow naturally.

51.

It's Okay to Change Your Mind

JUST BECAUSE you're the parent doesn't mean you won't be wrong from time to time. So it's important to be able to navigate the fine line between the power of parenthood and the humility of being fallible. Parents often make the mistake of digging in their heels and stubbornly refusing to be persuaded by a reasonable argument. They don't like to admit to a child that they might have been wrong.

Children need to see that it's natural to make mistakes from time to time (#44). The last thing you want is a child who is unable to own up to the fact that she was wrong. If you're trying to teach your kids to be open-minded and responsible for their actions, you must demonstrate this behavior yourself. How better to learn than from a parent?

Some parents believe their authority will be undermined or that it's a sign of weakness if they allow themselves to be swayed or to admit they've been wrong. With others it's often a false notion of how a parent should behave, or simply bad judgment. Whatever the cause, you're doing a disservice to your children by taking this position. And you complicate your life in the process.

As to your ability to stand firm in the face of an argument, what's the point? If your children come up with a better case than you have, and are able to reason with you, they learn that clear thinking and logic can prevail in the face of adversity. It teaches them to weigh their options and think responsibly.

Be proud of your kids when they present a reasonable case for their request. A good argument is a sign of a strong intellect. Your willingness to listen and be flexible is not a weakness. You haven't caved in, and it doesn't set a dangerous precedent. You're still the parent, but now you're wonderfully human, too.

Eight

CONFLICT

52.

Limit the Options

ONE OF THE REASONS parents want to simplify their lives is so they'll have more time with their kids. But so often what could have been quiet, enjoyable time together ends up in conflict. There are a number of ways you can prevent this.

One way is to limit the options. Parents often make the mistake of giving a child too many choices: "What would you like for breakfast?" or "What would you like to do today?" Too many choices can create problems, because younger kids still aren't able to realistically weigh their options and make a wise decision for themselves.

Children, who don't fully understand what the options are, get confused. Some kids want to do everything, and are reluctant to eliminate anything from their list of possibilities. Others get mad when you don't—or can't—go along with their choices: "But you asked me what I wanted to do today, and I want to go to Disney World!" If you've given them free reign, now you've got to deal with it.

Conflicts arise when kids make choices that aren't appropriate. What do you say when your child wants ice cream for breakfast, plans to wear pajamas to a birthday party, or decides today is a good day to go bungee jumping?

You can always respond with, "Wearing pajamas is not one of your options right now."

A simpler approach is to give your children a choice between two reasonable options that are both easy for you and that you know would appeal to them:

"Would you like cereal or waffles for breakfast?"
"Do you want to go to the beach today or help me in the garden?"
"Do you want to watch *Star Wars* or *101 Dalmations*?"
"You can wear your jeans or your khakis."
"Should I call David or John to come over?"

Choices can also be used for disciplinary situations:

"Do you want to get back by your curfew, or not go out at all?"
"Will you clean up the mess you made, or do you want to stay in your room?"
"Do you want to switch to *Sesame Street*, or should I turn the TV off?"

"Are you going to take turns playing with the Slinky, or do
you want me to take it away from both of you?"

"Will you put on some clean clothes before we go out, or
would you rather stay home?"

Start limiting choices when your kids are young so they don't
get used to having their own way with everything. And since you
have to commit to the choices you do offer, you want to make sure
they're ones you can live with.

53.

Don't Sabotage Yourself

THERE ARE MANY WAYS in which we sabotage ourselves as parents and make our jobs more complicated than they need to be. Here are some behaviors to avoid:

1. *Don't make promises you can't keep.*
   How many times have you talked about doing something with your children only to run out of time or find that you have to change your mind? You then end up arguing with your kids over how you never keep your promises. Share your plans with your kids only when you're absolutely certain you can fulfill them. Keep in mind that to a child a promise is anything you say you'll do or might do—it doesn't have to start with the words "I promise."

2. *Don't ask when there's no choice.*
   It took Tim a long time to learn not to undermine his requests in this way. He'd ask Andrew if he wanted to take a bath instead of telling him it was time for his bath. He'd ask Sasha would she please baby-sit Andrew while he ran an errand. He was trying

to be polite, but the kids ended up thinking they had a choice. They'd say no, and the inevitable struggle would ensue.

He's finally learned it's better to tell the kids what he wants them to do. "Please take the garbage out," and "Time to get ready for bed," leave no room for arguing. He may still get some resistance, but it's not as strong as when he gives them what they perceive to be a choice.

3. *Don't engage in an argument.*

Discuss things with your kids, reason with them, engage them in dialogue, but don't argue with them—it's a waste of time and energy. State your case, listen to their side of the story, reconsider your position if necessary, make your decision, and that's the end of it.

If they try to argue, walk away. It's hard to hit a moving target. If they follow you, restate your decision, and walk away again. Sticking around for an argument only prolongs it. Better to just physically remove yourself. (Go into the bathroom and close the door if necessary.) When you consistently show that you're committed to the decisions you make, your kids will eventually realize verbal harassment doesn't work.

And instead of nagging, use one-word reminders. "Dishes" or "bedtime" are clear messages that will avoid a prolonged discussion or argument.

4. *Don't hold a grudge.*

When your child does something wrong or hurtful, it's often hard to get over it and not to let it affect your future decisions or feelings. But you have to. Kids are spontaneous, whimsical creatures. They'll tell you you're horrible and mean when they don't get their way, then snuggle up with you the next moment and tell you you're the best mommy or daddy in the whole world. You've got to let go of the past as easily as they do. If you keep bringing up past mistakes and hurt feelings, you're setting up yourself, and them, for more conflict and disappointment. Deal with each issue as it comes up, then put it behind you. Forever.

5. *Don't give in under pressure.*

Children will push and push as long as they think there's any chance of getting you to change your mind and do it their way. Once they've stated their case, and you've made what you believe is the best decision, stick with it. If you give in, your children will learn that they can manipulate you—and they will.

Some kids will throw tantrums, others will argue or misbehave, still others will give you the silent treatment. If you consistently resist their efforts, firmly stay the course, and remember you're the parent, these behaviors will abate.

6. *Don't yell.*

I've said it before, but it bears repeating. Yelling and other forms of verbal abuse don't resolve anything; they only make matters worse. They're demeaning to children, deflect from the issue at hand, and teach that "might means right." A stubborn child will become belligerent; a shy one will withdraw in the face of anger. Remember, you're looking for a reasonable settlement, not an escalation of the conflict. Yelling shuts down dialogue just when you're trying to communicate.

7. *Always end on a positive note.*

Don't allow your child to leave the house or go to bed angry and upset. Do whatever you can to reconnect, firmly but lovingly, after an argument or an altercation. Let your child know that regardless of your temporary differences of opinion, you still love him and support him.

54.

Find a Third Party to Take the Heat

ONE GOOD WAY to avoid conflict is to deflect any part of the blame for an unpopular decision from yourself onto a third party. This would preferably be an authority that your child can't argue with and who will unknowingly bear the brunt of your child's frustration. Good third-party authorities include:

The doctor. When your child needs to take her medicine, have a dressing changed, eat more healthfully, or go to school when she's a little under the weather, blame the doctor: "I'm sorry, honey, but the doctor said you should go to school unless you're running a fever." (But never make the nurse or doctor appear scary or threatening in any way, or your child will resist the next visit to the doctor.)

The teacher. Invoke the teacher's name when you want your child to do his homework, study for a test, or finish a project on time: "I spoke to Ms. Farragher, and she said you should have the book report done by tomorrow morning. You'd better get busy."

The dentist. Dentists are good for anything having to do with dental hygiene or diet: "No, you can't have any candy. Remember what the dentist said about eating too many sweets."

Inanimate objects. A clock or an egg-timer is a great arbiter for taking turns, bedtime, bath time, and nap time: "Look, the clock says eight-thirty. I know you'd like to continue playing, but it's time for bed," or, "It's Kristen's turn when the timer rings."

And the chores list deflects a lot of emotional disputes over who's responsible for which chore. "It says right here it's Dan's turn to do the dishes."

One important exception to this rule is: Never blame anything on your spouse. That's adding marital conflict to the problems you're already having with your kids. And don't blame anything on an ex-husband or wife—it'll make a difficult situation worse, and the children will be the ones to suffer.

55.

Just Say Yes

ONE WAY TO AVOID conflict is to always try to say yes to your children's requests. Sounds impossible, but the twist is that it's a conditional yes. My mother used this approach for years and I always felt validated and listened to, even if I didn't always get what I wanted.

Here are some examples of how to respond to some common demands—ones that are usually met with an argument when they're refused with a flat-out no.

Child: "Can I have a cookie, please?"
Parent: "Sure, after you've finished your dinner."

Child: "Can I spend the night at Maria's?"
Parent: "Yes, that sounds nice—over the weekend sometime would be good."

Child: "Can we go to Disney World?"
Parent: "I'd love to! As soon as we find the time and save up enough money, we're on our way."

Child: "Can I have a new bike?"
Parent: "Great idea. Save up your money, and I'll drive you to the bike store and help you pick out your very own."

Child: "Can I stay up 'til midnight?"
Parent: "When you're fifteen, I'll consider it. But for now, ten o'clock is your bedtime."

Child: "Can I have a raise in my allowance?"
Parent: "We'll raise your allowance on your next birthday. Does two dollars more a week sound good?"

The idea is to turn the situation around to your advantage. There are several reasons this approach works better than a flat-out refusal.

First of all, you want your kids to have a positive attitude, so don't discourage their hopes. Saying yes leads to a dialogue rather than to an argument. Talk with them about how they can get what they want, and when they can expect to have it. Show them how to plan a trip, or shop for a good deal on a new bike; talk about how they'll spend their evenings when they can stay up until midnight.

Second, when you say yes, it's harder for them to argue, since you've just agreed with them. Be prepared for their likely reaction: a mixture of speechless confusion and frustration. Your kids will catch on to this trick eventually. But until they figure out what to say to a conditional yes, they'll usually just accept it. I did for years.

There will certainly be times when you'll have to say no, and that's fine. Kids need to learn how to accept no for an answer. When you do say no, make sure you mean it, and that you stick to it.

56.

Eliminate Tantrums

SOME KIDS SEEM TO SAIL through their childhoods without ever throwing a tantrum. Neither of Vera's sons had tantrums. They expressed their anger in other ways—Peter would cry for a while and then move on to the next interesting activity without looking back. Andrew would growl through gritted teeth, sulk for a while, and then get on with his life.

Sasha, however, made up for both of them in the tantrum department. From the age of one until about six, she threw a tantrum whenever she was frustrated. She had been such an easy, complacent baby that it took Vera and Tim completely by surprise.

When she had a tantrum, she would hit, bite, scream, and kick. It took some time to figure out why, when, and where she'd react with a tantrum, but as soon as they understood what set her off, they could avoid those situations.

They realized early that Sasha tired easily. When she was tired, she'd get cranky, and they found that's when tantrums were more likely to happen.

Sasha would go to bed quietly before 8:30, but if they waited until 9:00 to put her to bed, she'd fall apart. If they tried to separate her from an activity she was absorbed in, she'd have a tantrum; if they gave her fair warning and weaned her away, she was more likely to cooperate. She could also be distracted by another game or a funny joke.

Tantrums occur when kids are hungry, bored, or abruptly torn away from an activity. If your child tends to have tantrums, look for a pattern. It may take some time and effort on your part to figure out what works for your child. But because tantrums are exhausting for everyone, it's well worth the effort.

How should you react to a tantrum?

1. Don't give in. If you do, your children will learn that tantrums are a way to get what they want.
2. Make sure your child is safe, then simply walk away—tantrums need an audience.
3. If you're in public, physically remove the child from the situation.
4. Explain the consequences of a tantrum to your child—either a time-out, the premature end to a play date, or staying home instead of going on the next shopping excursion. Make sure the consequence fits the crime.
5. If your child throws a tantrum, wait until she calms down, then, assuming she's old enough to verbalize, talk to her about what happened. Find out why she was upset and explain why you

reacted the way you did. This will help you understand what set her off, and help prevent future tantrums. She'll begin to learn that tantrums don't work.

6. Help your kids understand and clarify their feelings. Teach children the word for what they're feeling. Kalin, the two-year-old daughter of a friend, would have tantrums when she tried to do something beyond her ability. Her mother taught her to say "frustrated." Now, instead of having a tantrum, she says, "Mom, I'm fusterated!"

7. Show your child an appropriate way to vent his anger—such as taking a time-out to pound his bed pillows. Explain to him in a quiet moment, not when he's already upset, that when he gets angry he can go into his room, close—not slam—the door, climb onto his bed, and pound the pillows furiously with his fists for a couple of minutes. Make it clear that he can't hit anything or anyone else with his fists or with the pillows.

57.

If Your Child Still Resists

HERE ARE SOME OTHER STRATEGIES you can try in the face of impending conflict:

1. *Give a warning.*
   Many conflicts arise when we want our kids to do something instantly and they just aren't moving fast enough for us. Imagine yourself engrossed in your favorite hobby and suddenly a huge giant comes along and drags you away to do whatever he wants to do. It would be very frustrating. A five-minute notice gives kids time to wrap up their game, finish their task, and get ready to make the transition to whatever happens next. This method works particularly well when you're getting ready for the school bus, calling your kids for mealtime, ending play dates, or getting ready for bed.

2. *Distraction.*
   Young children are eminently distractable. So the moment you sense conflict, simply divert your child's attention from the

source of their frustration to another activity. Say you want to end a game of Uno because it's bedtime. Rather than putting an abrupt end to their fun, invite them to join you for a story or something else you know they love. Sometimes it's as easy as pointing to something else and starting to talk about it.

If your child is getting cranky in the car, introduce a game of counting how many red cars they can spot. Or point out a dairy farm and talk about how cows are milked. Count the cows, make up an imaginary conversation two of the cows might be having, or tell a story about a day in the life of a little calf. Keep trying until you see that you've engaged your child.

Even when kids get older, they can still be easily distracted. Sasha loves a good joke, and Vera can get Peter's attention instantly by talking about boardsailing.

3. *Change your approach.*
One wonders why we invest so much effort in pursuing a course of action when it's obviously going nowhere. We start arguing, then argue more; yell, then yell louder; ground a child, then ground her for a longer period of time; impose a time-out, then stretch it out by a few more minutes. When it's clear the method doesn't work, try something else.

Stop for a minute, and then come up with another approach. If that approach doesn't work, try another one. Every child is different, so keep trying until you find what works for your child at this particular time.

4. *Use your secret weapon.*

If you reach a point in a conflict where you've tried everything—logical consequences, reasoning, distraction, changing tack—and you're still butting heads, then use their passion to get their cooperation.

With Peter it's the car. When he's mean to Sasha or belligerent with his folks, they warn him they'll take his car privileges away, and suddenly he's an angel. Sasha loves to ride and have sleep-overs with friends. If her parents even threaten to withhold either of these, she turns into the most compliant creature ever. Andrew loves *Sesame Street* and needs to snuggle at night, so those are the keys to getting him to behave.

It's never necessary to phrase it as a threat, but simply to say, in effect, "If you want our cooperation in helping you pursue your activity, then we expect your cooperation now." So, for example, you might say to your five-year-old who loves hugs, "If you want to snuggle with Mommy tonight, you have to go to bed now," or "Time for a snuggle—it's now or never."

5. *Discuss the problem.*

Children can be reasoned with, but not in the middle of a conflict. Wait a couple of hours, until everyone has cooled off, and then explain to your child how his behavior was inappropriate, find out what happened, and then, most importantly, discuss with him how you can avoid a repeat performance. The next time you're in a similarly difficult situation, remind him of your discussion.

58.

Minimize Sibling Rivalry

THERE ARE THOSE WHO SAY you can't eliminate sibling rivalry entirely, that often a sibling's mere existence is enough to start a fight. And certainly there are a number of factors that can contribute to the problem, including the ages of the siblings, their interests, personality differences, and the position of each in the family hierarchy. But there is much a parent can do to minimize the problem.

Obviously there will be unavoidable minor squabbles between siblings, in which the best course of action is to ignore them—or appear to ignore them—and let them work it out for themselves.

But I'm talking here about what can be done to eliminate the abusive, disruptive fighting between siblings that can make life miserable for the entire family.

One place to start is simply to insist that they get along. This doesn't mean they have to like each other at the moment, but they must be civil to each other. (You can acknowledge the feelings, without permitting the behavior: "I understand that you're upset with Taylor now, but you can't hit your brother.")

It means letting your children know that you'll tolerate nothing less than good behavior between them. It means being consistent (#43) and never letting them get away with fighting or name-calling. It means using time-outs (#42), separating them and sending them to their rooms, or imposing any other appropriate logical consequences (#41) when they fight.

And it means making it clear that you don't care who started it or why, but they'll each be dealt with seriously if they don't get along.

And there are other things you can do, too.

1. When your kids are young, don't let them get into the habit of fighting. Instead, start by showing them how to solve a problem that comes up between them. "Michael, you can color on the left side of the coloring book, and Sarah, you can color on the right side." Or, "Michael, you get to play with the train for ten minutes, then it's Sarah's turn." Set a timer, or let them set it. If they cry or make a fuss, take the book or the train away until they can play with it without squabbling. If you're consistent, they'll learn how to work it out themselves.

   As they get older, encourage them to look for their own solutions. Have them ask each other, "How can we resolve this so it's fair for both of us?" You may be happily surprised at the answers they come up with when they know they have to work it out themselves.

2. Don't play favorites. You might feel a greater kinship with one of your children than you do with the others. That's natural. It may require extra diligence on your part, but don't let this special connection influence your behavior toward them. Learn to appreciate each child for his or her particular strengths.

You'll also find there'll be times when one child is easier to get along with than the other, and then they'll switch—your sweet angel becomes belligerent and your uncooperative teenager takes out the trash without being asked. If you remain impartial, your kids will feel equally loved. But if you form an alliance with one, you're irrevocably hurting the other, and this only exacerbates the rivalry.

And a child who feels slighted because she thinks you're playing favorites may try to compensate by looking for negative attention—she gets to the point where she doesn't care whether you praise her or punish her as long as you're paying attention to her. In adolescence, this negative attention can be sought through promiscuous sexuality or drug use, and then life gets very complicated.

3. Resist the temptation to compare your children to each other— or to anybody else, for that matter. The comment "Why can't you be more like your little sister?" can easily end up with the little sister smugly looking down on her errant brother, and getting beaten up as soon as your back is turned.

4. Praise your kids in private. "What about me?" is the predictable refrain you hear when you praise a child in front of her siblings. The one that gets praised feels cocky and superior. The others feel slighted and unloved, even though that was not your intention. Give all of them encouragement at whatever they try to do, but find the time to do it privately.

5. Take your kids aside when you correct them, too. Being lectured or scolded in front of others is humiliating. For siblings it can be infuriating, and that fury can overpower any benefit that might have come from the correction. Never cause one child to feel good at the expense of the other.

6. When your kids are getting along well, sharing or cooperating in any way, praise them profusely. Make sure you let them know you've noticed, and how much you appreciate it. Then they'll each feel proud of having done something to please you.

7. Encourage siblings to help one another. This is sometimes easier to do when there is at least a three- or four-year age difference. When they're too close in skills and ability, they tend to compete rather than cooperate. But you can still find opportunities where siblings of any age can help each other—with homework, sports, chores, or simply sharing treats. If they feel they're on the same team rather than constant adversaries, they'll begin to get along better.

8. Be sure to take time to be with each child one-on-one. A family often becomes a chaotic and noisy place where the members are either pursuing their own agenda, fighting for attention, or getting lost in the crowd. You'll find a child can be quite a different person away from brothers and sisters—much friendlier, more affectionate, and often more cooperative.

You need to devote this kind of attention to each of them at least once a day, even if for a few minutes at bedtime. Better yet, making a regular weekly date with each child (#100) will go a long way toward eliminating problems between siblings.

59.

Look to the Future

SOMETIMES WE GET SO CAUGHT UP in a power struggle with our kids that we lose sight of what we're trying to accomplish. It's important to look beyond the immediate altercation to what we hope to teach our children in the long term.

Conflict brings out the worst in us. Our first impulse may be to get mad, yell, criticize, punish, flail our arms, swear, argue, look for someone to blame, assign guilt, slam doors, or throw things. But all these reactions only contribute to an escalation of the battle; they don't provide a resolution. Yell, and your kids will yell back. Criticism, blame, and guilt erode a child's feelings of self-worth. Arguing, swearing, and spanking are counterproductive and demeaning. All this behavior sets a bad example.

So what do you do? Once again, take a deep breath, or two or three, count to ten, then focus on the issue and concentrate on finding a solution.

Your son hit a ball through the neighbor's window: Is anyone hurt? Did anything else get broken? Have you spoken to the neighbor? Helped with the cleanup? Let's figure out how you're going to pay for this. Next time, play in the park.

Your six-year-old spilled paint on the carpet: Show her how to clean it up, and restrict painting to a safer area.

A belligerent child is irritating everybody merely for the sake of irritating everybody: Banish him to his room until he's ready to act appropriately.

Whatever the offense, tell your child, "This is the consequence of your behavior. I'm not interested in finding someone to blame. I'm interested in preventing this from happening again. From now on, we're going to do it this way."

Then describe to your child exactly what you expect the next time she encounters a similar situation: "Clean this mess up, and next time promise you'll paint at the kitchen counter."

"You can come out of your room when you can get along with everyone."

"From now on, if you want to make mud pies, do it outside."

"Next time you decide to go for a swim, take your shoes off first."

This way your energy is expended providing guidance rather than finding blame or blowing up. Conflicts are avoided, and mistakes become learning experiences.

Nine
FAMILY ISSUES

FAMILY ISSUES

60.

Make Parenting a Team Effort

FATHERS ARE MORE INVOLVED in the lives of their children today than ever before. Unlike the traditional image of the *Leave It to Beaver* family of a few decades ago, there are now part-time and full-time stay-at-home fathers, fathers who arrange their schedules around their children's activities, and dads who change diapers, get up in the middle of the night to comfort a colicky baby, take their kids to birthday parties, confer with teachers, and come home from work early if their child is sick.

Recent research at UCLA School of Medicine shows that children whose fathers are involved in their care tend to adapt better socially, are less likely to become violent, and have higher IQs.

But even though more mothers than ever are now working full time outside the home, just as fathers are, there is still a large number of fathers who, to their own loss and their kids' loss, are only minimally involved in the care of their children. There are any number of reasons for this, ranging from classic workaholism to the absence of role models. But, statistically, it's still the women who bear the brunt of the household and child-rearing responsibilities today.

If you're a mother in this position, address the problem with your mate. Careers and family make competing demands that can sometimes seem irreconcilable; but a father needs to understand that now is the only time to establish a relationship with his children—there is no later. He also has to realize that placing an undue burden on you just isn't fair. There's too much for one person to do, and you're both responsible for your children.

Here are some steps you can take to turn the situation around:

Start with a frank discussion, or a series of discussions. Many women are afraid of "bothering" their spouses with domestic stuff. But take some time to think about what you'd like your husband to contribute, and then talk with him about it.

Arrange for your husband to schedule regular time with the kids in the same way he schedules a business trip. Sit down together with your family calendar (#76) and go over next month's dates and appointments. Figure out which one of you will be responsible for what, which days will be best for him to be out of town or to work late, and which days he'll need to be home for your son's championship game or for teacher conferences. Obviously there'll be times he'll have to be away on a certain day, and then perhaps you can reschedule the event to fit his needs.

Clearly communicate what your needs are. Don't expect your spouse to magically read your mind, then be disappointed when he doesn't.

Create opportunities for your spouse to be alone with the kids. Arrange to leave the kids with their father on a Saturday or Sunday afternoon when you know he's free. He'll learn what it takes to care for the kids, and you'll get some time for yourself.

Don't criticize. When you hand your kids over to their father's care, don't be critical of what he does. They'll eat, but probably at McDonald's. They'll get dressed, but probably not in the outfits you'd have chosen. They'll go to bed, but probably after their regular bedtime. Make it easy for him when you leave, and keep your mouth shut when you return. It's the time they spend together that's important.

Encourage your kids to be responsible for their own relationship with their father. Often a mother will act as messenger between father and children. She asks him for things on their behalf, and then reports back to the kids. If your kids want or need something from their dad, have them ask him directly, and vice versa. This teaches the children to express themselves and to communicate with their father, and it makes him accountable for any promises he makes.

Get help with housekeeping. Close to 70 percent of mothers work outside the home, yet women are still 95 percent responsible for running the household. Get your husband to pitch in. Ask him which chores he'd like to be in charge of. Make it a multiple-choice question rather than a yes-or-no option. If he can't, or if you both feel overwhelmed with too many other obligations at the moment, hire someone to help with the housework until you can simplify some of the other areas of your life.

Children need both parents involved in their lives—as role models, playmates, teachers, advisers, friends, and caretakers. Do everything you can to make parenting a real partnership.

61.

Keep Your Family Together

EVERY MARRIAGE has its rocky years. There are few couples who haven't at some time questioned whether or not they should stay together. All too often they bail out before identifying problems that could have been resolved through patience, hard work, and marital therapy. A breakup can be painful at any time, but when children are involved, it's devastating.

The National Survey of Children reports that children of divorce are two to three times as likely to have emotional and behavioral problems as are children living with both parents. Divorce is one of the most common factors leading to developmental problems, teenage pregnancy, violent behavior, and drug and alcohol abuse. And parents and children of divorce suffer financial and lifestyle changes when assets are split and money becomes an issue.

Of course, if you're a victim of physical or emotional abuse, you have no choice but to get out of the relationship and save yourself and your children. If you feel there's still hope for the marriage, get counseling *after* you've separated—don't stick around hoping your spouse will change. You're endangering the physical, psychological, and emotional welfare of your children by remaining in a volatile or violent environment.

And there are some marriages that are simply unworkable because one party, or both, refuse to change, refuse to get help, or refuse to acknowledge that problems exist. There are parents who decide, and often rightly, that the environment their relationship creates is not one in which their children should be raised.

But if, like many couples, you've grown apart, you're angry or bored with your spouse, or you wonder if this is all there is, there's a strong possibility that the problem is not with the marriage but with your expectations.

Some people have bought into the myth that a couple can live happily ever after without any effort. But it's impossible to sustain a constant passion for your partner over decades of marriage, especially during the more exhausting, noisy, and stressful years of child-rearing.

Many couples lack the communication skills necessary for working out their problems, and grow angry and resentful when difficulties arise. Others pattern their marriage after their parents' marriage—and many of those were dysfunctional relationships.

It's not uncommon for marriages to undergo tension when the youngest child goes off to school. Until then, both parents are so busy juggling child care and work that there's no time or energy left to focus on the marriage. Suddenly, when all the children are out of the house, old issues and resentments surface.

If you're having marital difficulties, before you call the divorce attorneys consider these other options:

Put your children first. You've had your time, and you'll have time again when they're grown. Make this their time. Think seriously about how a divorce would impact their lives, not only on a day-to-day basis, but in the long term as well.

Understand that a divorce is only a physical separation—your ex-spouse will likely continue to play a big role in your life, possibly for the rest of your life. You'll still have to learn to get along in order to negotiate issues regarding your children. You might as well learn to communicate and address your problems while you're married, because you'll have to deal with them anyway.

Be certain you understand the economic consequences before you add financial problems, and the stress of dealing with children who desperately miss their noncustodial parent, to the already monumental challenges of raising kids.

This is absolutely not to say you should stay in a bad marriage for the sake of the children or for financial reasons. Rather, it's to suggest that you do whatever you can to make your marriage work for the sake of the children, and for your own sake.

Talk to your spouse—calmly, nonjudgmentally; communicate your feelings to each other.

Consult a good marriage counselor. But before you do, read *Divorce Busting,* by Michelle Weiner-Davis (Summit Books, 1992), to learn about a powerful, solution-oriented short-term therapy which you can use alone or with your spouse to save your marriage.

Don't make the mistake friends of mine made. They've been in intensive counseling, separately and together, for over three years. They've made little progress, they're marriage is still fragile, they've spent hundreds of dollars, and their children's lives have been in a constant state of upheaval. If you haven't made some discernible progress after a couple of months, the chances are good you picked the wrong counselor. Find another one.

Talk to friends who managed to save their marriage. Find out what they did to make it work. Many will tell you they're thankful they made the extra effort to stay together, and now their relationship is better than ever.

Talk to friends who chose divorce. You may be surprised at how many will tell you they wish they'd worked harder to save their marriage and to keep their family together.

Be patient. No doubt it took awhile for things to get bad. It may take awhile for them to get better.

In the meantime, get on with your life. Don't stew while you wait for your relationship to improve. Take up a sport, enroll in adult education classes, find work you like, do things with friends. Take responsibility for your own happiness and fulfillment. It's not your spouse's job to keep you amused.

Learn the skills required to sustain a relationship. Be realistic, and understand that unless you've honestly dealt with the issues that are causing the problems, second marriages—with step-parents, step-siblings, half-siblings, and all the other complications of step- and half-relatives—are not the panacea they're thought to be. Over fifty percent of second marriages end in divorce. That tells you something.

Do everything you can, and then some, before filing for divorce. If your marriage still doesn't work out after all that effort, at least you'll know you did your best.

62.

Dealing with Divorce

IF YOU'VE DONE EVERYTHING you can and still feel that divorce is the best solution, or if you're already divorced, how can you help your children make a successful transition into new lives and new family arrangements?

The best course is to stay on friendly terms with your ex-spouse. Obviously this is easier said than done, but no matter what has gone on between you, you still have children together, and you've got to be able to work together to raise them. Make your children's best interests your priority.

Never speak ill of your ex-mate in front of the children or ask them to take sides, no matter how angry and bitter you may be. Don't let them overhear conversations you have with others about how you really feel toward their parent, who may be taking you to court again over child support or visitation rights. Try not to burden your children with your feelings. Save the trauma you're going through for your therapist or your best friend.

As kids grow up they'll be able to judge whether a parent was fair, and whether one parent made it difficult for them to have a good relationship with the other parent. Children need to love both parents in order to live balanced lives and have healthy relationships with others in the future.

Honor your agreement when it comes to visitation, but be flexible when special events come up. Agree to switch weekends or to make changes as needed. The more access noncustodial parents have to their kids, the more likely they stay involved in their children's lives.

Do what you can to keep your children from experiencing dramatic upheavals. Stay in the same house or apartment and the same school district if you possibly can, so they can pursue the same activities and play with the same friends.

Explain to your children—over and over again, if necessary—that the two of you weren't getting along, but that you both still love them as much as ever. Realize that, depending on their ages and their personalities, many children simply won't understand that it wasn't their fault, and may suffer agonizing guilt over the breakup. Some kids worry about their parents and feel responsible for their happiness. They may internalize their own worries so as not to further burden their parents. Others act out in order to get the attention they need and want.

Get your kids to open up about their feelings. When you see they're anxious, depressed, or falling behind in school, get them to discuss what's worrying them. It's important for your kids to get proper closure, too. The first two years after a divorce are often the most difficult, especially for boys. Your kids may need counseling to help them through this difficult time in their lives. Or consider a school-based or community-sponsored support group for children of divorce. Kids feel more "normal" when they know other kids are experiencing similar situations.

At the same time, you have to make it clear to your children that you and your spouse won't be getting back together. In the kindest way possible, don't let them cling to a false hope that prevents them from getting on with their lives.

Encourage your children to communicate with their other parent, to see each other and talk on the phone as much as possible. Kids need both parents.

If you decide to start seeing someone else, leave your kids out of it until the relationship becomes serious. Kids can get very attached to new people, and then feel abandoned if it doesn't work out. An unsuccessful new relationship will complicate your life all over again.

Avoid overnight visitors when the children are in the house. It sends a confusing message to kids. They wonder if this new person will be take the place of Mom or Dad, or displace the affection Mom or Dad feels for them. As much as you want the company, consider your children first.

63.

Make Single Parenting Easier

RAISING CHILDREN requires extraordinary effort. Families with two parents at home have their hands full. The challenges can seem overwhelming to single parents. Everything—financial worries, loneliness, fatigue, problems with the kids—seems so much harder when you're facing it alone.

It's easy to advise and very difficult to do, but the first step toward simplifying is to let go of the anger or grief you may feel about being alone.

Whether it's divorce or the death of your spouse that has made you a single parent, you have to resolve your feelings and put the past behind you. Give yourself time to deal with the anger or mourn the loss of a loved one, get professional help if you need to, for yourself and your children—but keep your focus on the present rather than the past. If you allow your anger or grief to consume you, it'll make your job that much harder.

The key to being an effective parent is efficiency. And the key to being an effective single parent is being doubly efficient. You barely have the time and energy to deal with the kids, run the house, and hold a job. So what's the best way to manage it all and still have the time to enjoy your family?

Possibly the biggest step you can take to make single parenting easier is to find a job that gives you flexibility in terms of hours. Many employers now offer flextime, job sharing, and child-oriented time off.

Explore these possibilities with your present employer, or seriously consider a job change. Since you don't have a partner to take up the slack, you'll want to be in a work situation that'll make it easier for you to deal with sick days when you're stuck without a baby-sitter. You'll need to be able to take time off to attend parent-teacher conferences, your kids' school performances, doctor appointments, and any other things that have to be taken care of during normal business hours.

Another option you'll want to consider is to work at home (#67).

Make an extra effort to keep the lines of communication open with your kids, and be serious about disciplining them. Be sure to schedule time for fun. There'll always be jobs that need to be done around the house, but it's far more important to spend time with one another.

Schedule a day or two each month (and a few evenings, if you can) when you put aside your responsibilities, leave your beds unmade, the laundry unwashed, and simply have fun together. And it's more important now than ever that you take the time to nurture yourself (#8).

Take all the help you can get (#14)—from aunts, uncles, cousins, friends, neighbors, grandparents, and other relatives on both sides, as well as from any applicable federal, state, or local programs. Don't let pride stand in the way of improving your life or the lives of your children. Anything you can do to lighten your burden will benefit your family.

Join a support group for single parents. It's helpful to be able to share your feelings with people who understand. As much as your married friends may sympathize, they simply don't know what you're going through.

Stay focused on spending your time and energy on the people and the things that are most important to you—your children, your job, a few close friends, a special interest.

Don't shut out the world. It's easy to isolate yourself after a divorce or a death, but that will only prolong your loneliness and sadness. Make the effort to see friends, go to the movies, take a trip, meet new people, take up a hobby or a sport you've always been interested in. Create a new life instead of despairing over the loss of your old one.

Nobody expects you to forget the past, but you have to get on with your life, for your sake and the sake of your kids. Remember that your children will be looking to you for signs that everything is okay. It'll make life easier if you can convince them, and yourself, that it is.

64.

The Extended Family

STEPCHILDREN, ex-wives and ex-husbands, in-laws and former-in-laws, and half-brothers and -sisters make up a large part of many families these days. The dynamics of these blended families greatly affect a child's view of the world—a place that seemed so stable and safe when Mom and Dad lived together.

As a parent, it's your job to help the children feel secure about their new family and their home so they thrive socially, emotionally, and academically. Integrating two families is a difficult proposition; it can be a nightmare for everyone involved if not handled properly.

How children react to a second marriage depends on many factors. Younger children are more adaptable than older ones. Adolescents, who are just beginning to develop their own relationships, have the hardest time.

Girls seem to have less trouble adjusting than boys, but both have a difficult time accepting a stepparent of the same sex as themselves. As a stepparent with three stepchildren, you may get three different reactions, depending on the children's age, sex, and temperament: one may embrace you, another may be indifferent to you, and the third may be openly hostile.

Here are some ways to make the transition easier:

1. Let the parent parent. Make it very clear to the children that the stepparent will not replace their mother or father. If you're the parent, don't abdicate your duties by expecting the stepparent to take over your parenting responsibilities. Raising your kids is your job, not your new partner's.

   Also, if necessary, make it clear to the children that they will not be able to harass a stepparent into leaving.

   Although stepparents will sometimes have to do some disciplining, let the parent do as much of it as possible. Stepparents have a great opportunity to offer their stepchildren friendship and support. Stepparents can encourage the children's hobbies and interests, help them with their homework, teach them to cook or to sail, and be there for them when they're needed. Stepparents can assume the role of an older, kind, and caring friend, and let the parents deal with the confrontations and consequences.

2. Give the kids time with their parents. If you're the parent, make sure you arrange to have time alone with your children when their stepparent is not around.

   If you're the stepparent, you'll inevitably have to share your spouse with his or her children, whether you like it or not. Better to accept that fact, get used to it, and make plans of your own than to allow resentment to fester. In fact, encourage your spouse to spend time with his or her children. Remember that your happiness depends in large part on the happiness of other members of your extended family.

3. Establish house rules (#11). Your stepchildren now have two homes and they inevitably do things differently at each home. Make sure everyone understands the house rules in your home. It's easier if the children's parent discusses the rules and acts as the enforcer. The stepparent should help facilitate adherence to the rules, but it's not his or her job to be policeman, judge, or jury. That's the parent's responsibility.

4. Don't play favorites. If there's something special you want to do with your own kids, do it in private. Don't heap attention, praise, or gifts on your own children while your stepchildren look on, feeling left out. Stepchildren will assume that you have a special bond with your own kids and will accept some differences in treatment, but it's cruel to show blatant favoritism in your dealings with them.

5. Insist on respectful behavior. No matter how angry the children get about a remarriage or how they feel about their parents and stepparents, insist on discussing differences instead of yelling, slamming doors, or calling names.

6. Remember, it's difficult for the kids, too. As hard as it is for you to be part of a newly blended family, it's unfamiliar territory for the kids as well. They need to feel accepted and loved whether they're being good or bad—just as they were loved in their original family. And they're going to test the limits of a step-parent the same way they do their parents.

   Don't forget you're the adult. You have to respond with logic, consistency, good humor, and great patience, while being firm and maintaining your composure.

7. Don't give up. In one family I know, the three-year-old daughter accepted her stepfather as if he were her father from the very beginning. Her six-year-old brother, however, had a more difficult time relating to this new person in his life, and the stepfather quickly gave up on ever winning the boy over. If the stepfather had tried harder, there's a good chance the boy would have eventually come around and accepted him.

8. Take a stepparenting class. Many schools and communities offer stepparenting classes that provide information, understanding, and an opportunitiy to share experiences with others. Simply knowing there are other stepparents who are experiencing similar challenges is a big help and relief.

9. Be especially sensitive if a new baby arrives. Don't make too much of a fuss over the new baby when the other kids are around. Continually reassure the older kids—not only verbally, but by

your actions—that the baby does not displace them or threaten their safety or security in the family. You can't go wrong if you're fair, consistent, attentive, and loving with all your children and stepchildren.

65.

Know Your Child Care Options

THERE'S NOTHING SIMPLE about finding good child care. You may leave your children for an hour or for the entire day, but the care they receive has to be the best available. This is a real challenge, given that studies of the child care industry have shown that only 40 percent of commercial centers meet even the minimum requirements for basic care.

Your children are the most precious people in your life. It's not enough to look for a caretaker who "speaks English, has a driver's license, and is a nonsmoker." You also want someone with experience, patience, maturity, good references, and, most importantly, someone who loves children—your children in particular.

You can make the process of finding good child care easier by understanding your options and knowing how to properly evaluate a provider.

Here is a list of possible child care providers and some things to consider with regard to each one.

In your home:

Relatives have a vested interest in your child and often they don't charge for their services. But they may not consider it a serious job and may not be available when you need them most. And, in truth, there are no free lunches, so realistically evaluate the cost.

Live-in nannies and au pairs are available round the clock and provide a sense of stability for your kids—although most will only work on a year-to-year basis. But they're expensive; you lose your privacy; and the odds are high that you or your children won't like them. Most often the best nannies are daughters of friends or family. Going through a nanny agency does not insure that you'll get along any better than if you advertise for a nanny yourself.

Baby-sitters can provide stability for your kids; they come and go as you need them; you pay only for the hours worked; and you retain your privacy. But they may not be available when you need them, and they tend to be expensive.

There are now devices that make it possible for parents to spy on their baby-sitters via a hidden camera housed in a teddy bear. Many caregivers who have been spied on have been fired after parents watched how they interacted with their children— or how they failed to interact by spending hours on the phone or in front of the TV while ignoring the kids.

Whether you choose a relative or a baby-sitter, make sure the caregiver has a good relationship with your children and stimulates and actively plays with your kids rather than planting them in front of the TV. Drop in unexpectedly to see what they're doing. Ask your kids if they like the caregiver. Ask what they did during the day. And watch for signs that things aren't working out, like sudden changes in your child's behavior.

Outside the home:

Child care centers are less expensive than private care and provide your child with an opportunity to interact with other kids and play with different toys. Operators need to be licensed and meet minimum standards. But they're not available for sick children; your child may get lost in the crowd; toys may be inappropriate for your child's age; and there's frequently a high turnover in staff.

Child care in the caregiver's residence is less expensive than child care centers or private care, and the caregiver is constant from year to year. Your kids sometimes have other kids to play with and a limited number of toys. But these providers may not be licensed, and they are loosely regulated. They may exceed the recommended ratio of children to adults, and the caregiver need not be trained.

Preschools are relatively inexpensive, allow lots of social interaction with other kids, have educational materials on hand,

and must be licensed by the state to meet minimum requirements for health, safety, and teacher/student ratio. But you're restricted to the hours the school is in session, which is usually only a few hours a day and none on holidays.

Here are some questions to ask when looking for quality care outside the home. Remember, you'll be leaving your child in this place for many hours a day, day after day. "Adequate" isn't enough of a requirement—it must be a nurturing environment as well.

1. *The physical plant:* Is it bright and airy? Is it clean and safe? Are the bathrooms clean? Are cabinets locked and is the yard fenced in? Would you like to spend a day in this place?
2. *The staff:* Are they trained? How long have they worked there? How frequent is the turnover?
3. *Individual caregivers:* Are they sensitive to the kids? Do they speak to your child directly? Do they give each child one-on-one attention every day? Do they play with the kids? Do they help resolve problems, or do they yell and punish the kids? Are they open to your questions and concerns?
4. *Adult/child ratio:* How many adults watch how many kids? Make sure the state-mandated guidelines for various ages are not exceeded.

5. *Age:* Are children separated by age? You don't want a four-year-old in the same area as an infant or toddler—their care, interests, and abilities are widely divergent. A caregiver can't meet all their needs and still provide adequate time for play and nurturing.

6. *Toys and activities:* Are they age-appropriate and stimulating? Are the toys and climbers in good shape? Does the center acquire new playthings from time to time?

7. *Cost:* Are you getting good value for your money? Be prepared to pay more to get better care. Recent surveys of the child care industry have shown that often even a slightly more expensive center will give you a lot more in terms of the quality of care.

8. *Accessibility:* Can you drop in anytime unannounced? These visits give a true picture of what your child's day is like. Don't even consider a center that doesn't allow you access to your child at any given moment.

Most importantly, you have to listen to your heart and to your children, even if it means having to go through the hassle of finding someone new to watch your kids.

66.

Consider Working from Home

THERE IS NO SUBSTITUTE for an at-home parent in a child's life. No matter how good the child care you provide, your child's passion is for you, the parent. If you've never considered it before, think about working from home.

You can find a creative solution for earning the income you need while being available for your kids. There are more opportunities than ever for at-home careers. Computer work, desktop publishing, proofreading and graphics; landscape design; architecture, engineering, and drafting; tutoring; writing and editing; medical, counseling, and consulting practices are among the many possibilities.

Think about how much simpler it would be to work from your home. You wouldn't have to worry about day care, transportation to and from after-school activities, days when the baby-sitter gets sick, or evenings when your boss wants you to work past your children's bedtime. You'd have more time to give your children the attention they need, to be involved with their academic and extracurricular activities, and to supervise their free time.

You may have to change your lifestyle and give up some material things, but it may be worth it.

When Vera learned she was pregnant with Peter she wanted to be a stay-at-home mom, but she and Tim needed her income. Her job as promotion manager at a national sports magazine involved working with various freelancers—photographers, graphic designers, illustrators, sales reps. She'd always enjoyed design and decided to pursue that interest. She was able to make arrangements with her employer so she could become a home-based graphic designer once the baby arrived.

During her pregnancy she studied graphic design and was able to step into her new part-time, working-from-home position after Peter was born. It worked out well for everyone—it just took a little creative engineering. Many employers are open to shared jobs, flexible hours, and other options that make it possible for parents to work from home.

Consider working from home even if you're the primary breadwinner—either full-time or one or two days a week. For years I went to a family dentist who had his dental office in his home. He had his staff schedule his appointments around his children's activities.

A home office gives you the benefit of being near your family, and you gain the time you would otherwise lose commuting. Most importantly, you're at home when your children need you, and you get to share in the joys of their childhood years.

While a home-based job can potentially give you more time with your kids and a flexible schedule, it also requires a lot of self-discipline and good organizational skills. You need to think carefully about whether this would be a viable solution for you right now. If it is, it could really simplify your life with your kids.

67.

Think About Becoming a Full-Time Stay-at-Home Parent

RECENT RESEARCH conducted at the University of California at Berkeley shows how important it is for one parent to be the primary caregiver for at least the first three years of a child's life. Even if the child care one finds is ideal, which it seldom is, there's still no substitute for hands-on parenting.

Parents need to be there to hold and cuddle their infants, to walk with and talk with their toddlers, and to provide love, care, stimulating experiences, and guidance for all their kids. And parents are the only ones who can pass on their family values to their children.

There are obviously circumstances, such as being a single mom or dad, that would make being a full-time stay-at-home parent an impossibility. And there are also many parents who are under either financial or career pressures at the moment that make full-time parenting an unrealistic option. In these situations, there are many other things you can do, including organizing your weekends around your family (#7) or working from home (#66) that will help provide your children with much of the parental contact they need.

But many parents are starting to make changes in their lifestyles so at least one parent can be at home with their kids full-time.

Mothers are setting more realistic expectations about the kinds of careers they can pursue, at least during the child-rearing years. Fathers are opting for less stressful work lives; they're working closer to home or at home so they can eliminate long commutes. Some dads are choosing to be the one to stay home part-time and even full-time to be with their kids.

Many parents are changing their ideas about the trappings of so-called success that have made it seem necessary for both of them to work full-time outside the home. They're learning it is possible to live on one salary.

I frequently hear from parents who've decided not to have a bigger house, who've found they don't have to drive the latest model car, and who've discovered inexpensive ways to entertain their families and provide for their basic needs.

If it's your heart's desire to stay at home to be with your kids, and if you're thinking you'd like to try living on one income, here are some things to consider:

1. Set up a budget—and live by it, year after year. I know; budgeting is a tedious word, and most people don't like to even

think about it. But a budget is your blueprint. If you don't know how much money you have coming in or where it's going, living on only one salary will be more difficult.

2. Make sure that no more than 25 percent of your income goes to pay for your housing costs. Yes, this may mean a smaller house, sometimes in a less-expensive neighborhood. But if it's a choice between living in a big house and spending time with your kids, there really is no choice.

3. Adopt the policy that if you don't have the cash in hand, you can't afford it. With the exception of your home and possibly your car, don't buy on credit. At the very least, buy a second-hand car to help keep your car payments manageable.

   If you're unable to pay your credit cards in full each month, cancel your cards. Cut them into pieces and throw them away. Then establish a plan to pay off any existing credit card or consumer debt balances within the year.

4. Learn to disregard the messages from television, magazines, newspapers, and other media that create consumer needs for you, and particularly for your kids.

5. Check local consignment shops or garage sales before you buy anything retail.

6. To minimize the stuff that complicates your lives and puts you into debt, don't buy *anything* but food and the absolute necessities for the next thirty days. After you've done it for a month,

commit to it for another month. Then commit to it for a year. Trust me on this. You can do it. I've done it for years. And I hear from many people who are breaking their spending habits by taking similar steps.

7. Allow yourselves a night out every now and then. Don't deny yourself the little pleasures you and your family enjoy, but keep it simple and stay within your budget. And don't overlook activities that are relaxing, entertaining, and fun that don't cost anything.

8. Take your vacation at home this year. And possibly next year. And possibly for several years after that. Use the time to relax and be together without the pressure of work, and without the stress of going into debt for a trip to Disneyland. Or find ways to get away that don't cost a lot of money, such as camping trips or inexpensive day trips to nearby areas of interest.

9. Don't spend your next raise. Or the one after that. And possibly not the one after that. And don't spend your bonuses either. Put them into a college fund or into your retirement account.

You may be surprised, once you rearrange your thinking and break your consumer habits, how easy it is to live well without spending a lot of money. And getting out of debt, staying out of debt, and knowing that you're building a solid financial foundation will give you a sense of power and freedom that few other things can provide.

If the idea of full-time parenting seems daunting, take a parenting class or two or three, and read books on child rearing. These things will open your mind to new methods as well as the time-tested ways of parenting. And meeting other parents who are experiencing the same challenges will make your life easier.

Many working parents struggle to connect with their kids because they're not in sync with their children's current interests and development. But as a stay-at-home parent you'll quickly establish a closer bond with your kids. You'll find that the more you parent, the better you get at it, and the easier it becomes.

Arranging your lives so one of you can be with your kids—and so that you can both devote your energy to being the best parents you can be—requires dedication, planning, and effort. But if you're approaching parenting as the most important career you'll ever have, it'll make fulfilling that career goal a whole lot simpler.

Ten

SIMPLE HOLIDAYS
AND CELEBRATIONS

68.

Make Holidays Easier

THE EXCITEMENT AND JOY that kids bring to holiday festivities
are high on the list of reasons people continue to keep those traditional celebrations alive. And there's something about the *idea* of
the holidays that appeals to the kid in all of us. But if, like many
parents, you find that the commercialism and excesses of the holidays complicate your life, here are some ideas for celebrating them
differently.

1. Set limits on gifts. Give only one or two special gifts to each
   child and perhaps a couple of small presents, especially if your
   kids have grandparents and relatives adding to their stash.

   Rather than overwhelming your children with more stuff
   they'll soon tire of, teach them that the holidays are not about
   spending money you don't have on things they don't need.
   They're an opportunity for friends and neighbors and family to
   share in the spirit of love and togetherness.
2. Teach your kids to make gifts for one another, or encourage an
   older child to give a favorite toy he has outgrown to a younger

sibling or to another child who would love to have it. Or have each child come up with a list of imaginative things he'll do for his siblings—and his parents: a week of computer lessons for a younger sister; a free car wash for Dad; an afternoon of baby-sitting for Mom. Each item can be listed on a hand-decorated card, which can then be wrapped individually in a creative gift package.

3. Encourage your kids to make gifts or to give some of the clothes they no longer wear or toys they no longer play with to children in need. Most communities have toy drives or fund-raisers to help children whose families need assistance.

4. Cut back drastically on television viewing in the months prior to Christmas to avoid the toy commercials. The less often your kids are exposed to bed-wetting dolls and gaudy plastic weapons of destruction, the easier it will be for you to keep them satisfied with meaningful gifts they treasure.

5. If you have a large extended family, rather than having every-one spend time, energy, and money buying gifts for everyone else, draw names so that each person is responsible for only one gift. Set a limit on the dollar amount to be spent.

6. Encourage gifts of time spent together, or tickets to a special event—a concert or sporting event—that the recipient would enjoy. Not only does this greatly reduce the amount of stuff that clutters up your home, your lives, and ultimately the envi-

ronment, but it increases the time you spend with family members you might not otherwise see that often.

7. If you're the family member responsible for preparing the traditional holiday dinner, this year plan to do only as much as you can comfortably handle.

Don't host a seven-course sit-down dinner when a simple buffet will do.

Buy a delicious "homemade" apple pie instead of slicing, dicing, and baking all day or late into the night.

When guests offer to help or bring something, take them up on their generosity. Let go of trying to do it all.

Don't be shy about asking overnight guests to pitch in and wash up, cook a meal, or run an errand. Playing host or hostess doesn't mean being a slave or a martyr. Guests who appreciate your hospitality will happily lend a hand. If they don't—well, you'll know whom to eliminate from next year's guest list. As often as possible, invite people you genuinely like instead of people you feel you *should* invite.

8. Get outside help before, during, and after a large party—either a responsible neighborhood teenager or a professional catering service—to alleviate the work and stress. It can be well worth the cost.

High school baby-sitters can watch small babies during holiday meal preparations. Your older kids can help with the preparation and cleanup.

9. If attending parties makes holidays stressful for you, this year cut the number by half or more.

Unless you enjoy doing it all, which most of us admit we don't, then set your limit and stick to it: "Thanks so much, but we're simplifying the holidays this year, and will be doing only family events."

With a little planning and forethought it's possible to enjoy the holidays without having to deal with exhaustion, frayed nerves, and overextended charge accounts.

69.

Keep Birthdays Simple

HAVING LARGE NUMBERS of children armed with cake and soda wreaking havoc through the house is probably not high on any parent's wish list for simple living. Fortunately, it's possible to arrange easy birthday celebrations for your kids, and to enjoy yourself in the process. Here are some ideas to consider:

1. Start by limiting the number of participants. The same number of guests as the age of the child is a good rule of thumb.

   Even though everyone else is doing it, don't feel obliged to invite your child's entire class of twenty-five to a birthday party. This is just too many kids. Not only does it get expensive very quickly, but the party can easily get out of control.

   Also, big parties tend to overstimulate a child. With too much noise, too many bodies, and too much chaos, a young child can quickly become tired and cranky and end up in tears.

2. Organize your own activity at home.

   Often the simplest and least expensive party is one that you host yourself with no outside help, or with another mother who is willing to pitch in. Simple activities kids like include watching favorite movies, swimming parties, nature walks, and camping in the backyard.

Slumber parties or sports parties, with teams playing football or basketball, are other options.

Be sure to plan every second, especially parties for younger children, and announce ahead of time when the party will be over. Two hours is plenty of time for a successful party. Have other mothers or family members available to supervise. Otherwise, a lot of damage can be done if kids stay too long. In the presence of a receptive audience a usually responsible child can turn into a ruffian and become a pied piper, leading other kids to destructive behavior that will quickly complicate your day.

3. In the spirit of simple living, come up with ideas for keeping the kids happily occupied without having to hire caterers, ponies, jungle gyms, or bouncy castles. Consider buying tickets to the theater, a concert, or the circus. Offer your child a special treat with one or two friends instead of a party.

4. Consider having the party outside your home at a local park, on the beach, or in a community building if you have access to one. This causes the least amount of disruption to your home, and eliminates the juice stains on the sofa.

Other places that commonly host parties include museums, YMCA's, movie theaters, bowling alleys, restaurants, and nature centers. Though they can be more expensive, your only obligations for a party like this are to send out the invitations, provide the transportation, and police the participants. Again, enlist one or two of the other mothers to help supervise—and be prepared to return the favor.

5. Don't feel you have to have a formal birthday party for each child every year, or that a party must be held on your child's actual birthday. You could have special parties when your child turns three, five, and eight, for example, and have quiet family celebrations for the in-between years. This will help you avoid having to plan two or three parties each year if you have two or three young children of party age. Also, parties are more special and memorable for the child when they're not overdone.

6. Drop out of the competition for the "party with the best party favors" award. If you have party favors, keep them simple. Vera had a jewelry-making party for Sasha, at which the kids strung beads and made necklaces and bracelets, which became their favors.

Avoid the plastic bags filled with a marker, a candy, some stickers, and a cheap yo-yo that breaks the first time it's used. Better to invest in one good party favor that the child can enjoy for a while: a big rubber ball for each child with her name written on it in permanent ink; a set of colored markers; a blank book to use as a journal.

And you don't need all the other stuff stores sell for parties, like hats, whistles, and matching cups, plates, napkins, and favors.

7. Don't insist that your child go to every party he gets invited to. Andrew decided on his own when he turned five that there were only two parties he wanted to go to—his cousin's and his best friend's. He says no to everything else, and this has greatly simplified their lives.

8. Consider an alternative to birthday parties. I heard from one family who celebrate rites of passage—such as when a child graduates from third grade or learns to ride a bike—instead of birthdays. This way you're celebrating an accomplishment rather than the passing of time.

70.

Give Simple Gifts

FINDING SIMPLE but interesting gift for the kids in your life or for other kids can be a real challenge. Here are some ideas:

1. *Add to a collection.*

   Kids with collections are easy to shop for. Adding to a child's favorite set is a safer bet than picking a toy at random. Common collections include: LEGO, train sets, wooden blocks, dollhouse furniture, doll clothes, movie videos, and books.

2. *Key into an interest.*

   Make note of special interests. All kids have them. Do they like music? Buy them a CD or concert tickets. Skiing? Gloves, goggles, or other gear are a good bet. Sports? An autographed photo of a favorite sports star, tickets to a game, or a team shirt. Most kids love to draw or sculpt, so art supplies are always welcome gifts.

3. *Give homemade presents and cards.*

   My friend Kate keeps a supply of white unlined index cards on hand, on which her kids can draw a picture and write a personalized greeting. In spite of the fact that she lives in an area where there is great pressure to compete for the best gift, the best wrap, and the best Hallmark card, Kate's kids have always made their own gift cards and gift wrap for birthday presents, and frequently they make their own gifts for friends. Making cards on the computer is also fun.

Give a painting; a handknit sweater or scarf; a dress-up box with old clothes, hats, and jewelry; or an art or hobby box filled with creative projects.

Have your children help make a hostess present of freshly baked cookies, cake, or home-grown berry jam.

While handmade presents can be more time-consuming and might require more effort than purchasing a gift, they are also more special—to you and the recipient. People love receiving homemade presents because they include the gift of your precious time and thoughtful effort. One of the reasons to simplify is to free up time for more meaningful activities. Making gifts is something you can do together when you have your date with your child (#100).

4. *Consider these gift ideas as an alternative to toys:*

A contribution to a charity in the child's name

Money, gift certificates, stocks or bonds

Tickets to the movies, a concert, or a play

Ski lift tickets, admission to a zoo, a pass to a state or national park, or a minivacation, such as a trip to a nearby city to visit friends or relatives.

5. *Do what a friend of mine does with coins.*
On December 26 each year Randy starts saving his pocket change. By the next December 25 he has filled two large Mason jars with coins. He gives one jar to each of his two nephews, who have been awaiting it eagerly all year. They're occupied for hours on Christmas day counting out the money, and they've spent months beforehand joyfully contemplating what they'll spend it on.

6. *Make shopping easy.*
If you feel you must buy gifts, shop ahead of time so you don't end up in a frantic last-minute crunch. As much as you can, shop by catalog so you can avoid the hassles of driving, traffic, and parking. Buy in volume when there's a sale on practical items, such as art supplies or books.

Eleven

AT SCHOOL

71.

Play an Active Role in Your Child's Education

THERE ARE MANY WAYS to become involved in your children's life at school. Your involvement will dramatically increase your kids' chances for academic success, and when they succeed in school, your life and theirs become simpler.

Here are some things to consider:

1. Perhaps the easiest and most effective way to keep in touch with a child's progress in school is to volunteer as a room mother or father. This will give you the opportunity to help the teacher with class parties; art, history, and theater projects; and whatever other activities the teacher needs assistance with. Obviously, volunteering during the day is more difficult to do if you're working full-time, but it *is* still possible. Many employers permit child-related time off.

   Frequent contact with the teacher gives both of you an opportunity to closely monitor your child's progress throughout the year. Problems are nipped in the bud, and are much easier to deal with.

2. Volunteer as a chaperone when your child's class goes on an excursion. If you're employed full-time and your boss is not amenable to family-oriented time off, consider taking several vacation days or personal days as needed. You'll meet and get to know the children your child spends time with, and you can observe your child among his peers.

3. Stay on top of your child's academic performance. Get a copy of his schedule so you know what courses he's taking and who his teachers are. Meet the principal and the guidance counselor. Get updates on his progress. If there's a problem, voice your concern as soon as possible to the appropriate person.

4. Stay informed about future events. Learn who your child's teachers will be next year. Find out from other parents if they're good teachers. If you get reports that a teacher is mediocre, keep close tabs on how your child relates to him or her. If a problem arises, bring it to the attention of the administration immediately, and request a change.

As your children get older, schools offer exciting options like field trips or study abroad that must be signed up for months in advance. College testing, interviews, and applications all have deadlines. Don't miss sign-up dates.

5. Attend your children's class exhibits and school performances. Children work hard acquiring new skills and abilities. They

need the enthusiastic support of their parents. When you're cheering them on, it gives them the incentive to continue their interests. And it helps insure their continued success and independence.

72.

Help Your Kids with Their Homework

YOUR CHILDREN are learning something new and challenging every day. Whether they're absorbing a new concept or establishing proper study habits, most kids need help with their studies at one time or another. It's much easier to stay on top of your children's homework from the beginning than it is to play catch-up in the middle of a semester or halfway through their academic career.

Arrange for a quiet place where your kids can get their homework done without interruptions. A desk in their own room, or a table in a living or family room are possible options. Or arrange for them to study at the kitchen counter when you can be available to help if they have a question. This may also mean you'll have to minimize the distractions from phone calls, meal preparations, and playful preschoolers.

The first rule about homework, which should be established from day one, is that chores and homework come first. School assignments have to be completed before your kids can play with a friend, watch TV, or get involved in any other activity.

Provide the basic tools your children will need in order to excel academically, such as an encyclopedia, a good dictionary, and a computer. The computer helps with editing, spelling, research, and graphics. An encyclopedia and a dictionary are invaluable for quick reference. Get your kids into the habit of reaching for the dictionary or other reference books. Set that example yourself by consulting the appropriate reference book whenever a question comes up you don't know the answer to.

Have colored markers, good paper, white posterboard, and glue available for projects.

Review your child's work when she's finished. Help in whatever areas need improvement. Be sure you know what your child is currently studying. You'll be better prepared to help if you understand the material to be covered for each of your child's subjects.

Talk to the teacher if you start to see a downward slide. Maybe your child needs extra help in the classroom. She might need more time for her homework, or possibly private tutoring. Find out about special help that may be available through the school.

If your child has a big project, sit down with her and brainstorm an appropriate plan to complete it. Help her assemble the resources and supplies she'll need, outline the various options, and stand by to help while she pulls it all together.

On shorter projects and papers check spelling, grammar, and punctuation for her.

Don't criticize your child's efforts, and if she doesn't want your help on a project, that's her prerogative—don't force the issue.

None of this is to say you should do your children's homework for them, but it will greatly enhance their learning if you're there every step of the way advising, helping, or just observing. Your kids will learn to set high standards for themselves, they'll take pride in the work they turn in, and their achievements will become the foundation of their ultimate independence—and yours.

73.

Encourage Creativity

WHEN OUR CREATIVE SPIRIT is active it affects our whole way of being. A creative mind is one that sees a hundred possible solutions to a problem where a less creative mind may see only one—or none. A creative child has an easier time in school and is better prepared to succeed later in life.

Creativity and the willingness to solve problems, find innovative solutions, and work toward their dreams motivated such great thinkers as Leonardo da Vinci, Marie Curie, Thomas Edison, and Albert Einstein as well as modern inventors and innovators such as Bill Gates, Martha Graham, Georgia O'Keeffe, and Steven Spielberg.

Most schools teach conventional curricula and measure success by the results of standardized tests that all students are required to take in one grade or another. These are useful when a child has to transfer from one school to another, and they ease transitions from one grade to the next.

But standardization seldom rewards creativity. Tests are based on performance in academic areas like reading and math without any regard to abilities in art, music, or the performing arts; teachers are in a hurry to teach the required curriculum for the grade, and often don't have the time for enrichment programs that focus on creative thinking or problem solving; and school budgets are stretched to the limits.

All children have the potential to be creative. They love to draw, tell stories, play make-believe games, and find solutions to challenges. Standardized teaching, burned-out teachers, and budget cuts that affect arts programs all take their toll on a child's creativity by the second grade. It's often entirely up to you to nurture your children's creative spirits in addition to helping them with their required schoolwork.

Here are a few ideas on how to do this:

1. Show them how to illustrate their homework. Whether it's a science project, a book report, or history homework, a picture is often worth a thousand words. Maps, photographs, or other graphics can all be used to enhance assignments and projects.
2. Help your children think of interesting and innovative ways to tackle assignments in subjects they find boring. If they're assigned a math problem, use baseball or other sports statistics to solve it. For book reports and current events, have your kids ask if they can read about subjects they like, such as boardsailing, dinosaurs, or quantum physics—whatever sparks their interest.

3. Ask the teacher—or encourage your child to ask the teacher—if some assignments can be fulfilled by doing a skit, making a painting, or some other method that utilizes your child's abilities. If you have a child who is visually oriented, for example, creating a political cartoon might be more educational for him than writing a political essay. Teachers are often open to creative solutions to assignments that have become mundane for them.

At the same time, keep creativity alive at home.

1. Have lots of art supplies available, and make an art corner in your house. Don't skimp on art materials and don't worry about your children making a mess—simply require that they clean up after they complete a project.
2. Read stories aloud together and discuss the characters, plot, and development. Speculate on how the authors might have created their stories and their characters. Talk about how a different ending would change a story. Make up different endings. Do the same for movies you watch together.
3. Make up your own stories with your child—not only bedtime stories, but also stories you can build together on long car trips or while waiting in a doctor's office.
4. Discuss how great people became great. Examine what drove them to succeed, what obstacles they overcame, what their achievements were.

5. Discuss possible solutions to real problems. If you're having a hard time juggling your schedule, or your spouse has a challenging problem at work, or some domestic problem develops that needs attention, ask the kids to contribute their ideas toward workable solutions. Consider their contributions seriously, and have them help you implement their suggestions so they, and all of you, have an opportunity to see what works and how things can be made better.

74.

Don't Let Failure Be an Option

LOGICAL CONSEQUENCES can be used in many areas of a child's life, but allowing a child to fail at school to show her the consequences of bad grades seldom works. Because it's so public and humiliating, failure in school is poison to a child's self-esteem. Failing grades rarely teach a child how to succeed—they usually beget more failure. It then develops into a pattern that can be exceedingly difficult to overcome.

A child who fails in school begins to believe she's stupid, incapable, and no good. She gets a reputation for being a bad student, and lowers her expectations for herself based on her previous failures. She hangs out with other "losers" because she doesn't feel so bad around them. In the worst-case scenario, she drops out of school because she's tired of feeling bad about herself, and she does drugs in order to feel better.

You might think it's the teacher's responsibility to notice when your child isn't doing well, and then to take whatever steps are necessary to get her back on track. Unfortunately, it doesn't work that way. Most public school teachers have up to thirty kids in each of their classes. In middle school and high school, teachers teach up to six classes a day. That's one hundred eighty children a day.

If your child begins to lose interest in school, turns homework in late, falters on tests, drops from As to Bs and Cs in a subject, or begins to show any other signs of impending failure, it's a rare teacher who will even be able to see the slide, let alone avert it. You're responsible for making sure your kids are doing the best they're capable of doing.

Monitor your child's homework on a regular basis and talk with her about her progress and what she's learning in school. The moment you suspect your child might be stumbling, investigate. Find out if she's behind in her homework, if she missed a test, or if she talks too much in class. Put in a phone call to the teachers, and meet with them if necessary.

Perhaps your child has a learning disability and needs to be tested. Maybe she needs glasses or has a hearing problem. Maybe she's having a hard time socially. It's possible the teacher simply doesn't like her. Ask your child; you may find that somewhere along the way she got confused about the subject matter, didn't turn in a homework assignment on time, or was absent the day an important concept was explained. Or it could be one of a dozen other possibilities.

Your kids are still too young and inexperienced to handle these situations on their own. It's so easy for a child to jump to the conclusion that she's dumb, bad at math, can't learn how to spell, isn't creative, or will never be able to learn a foreign language. It's up to you to closely supervise your children's academic life, and to steer them toward success.

75.

Be Your Child's Greatest Advocate

PETER WAS A WHIZ in math in fourth grade. He was recommended for an honors math class in fifth grade, and was looking forward to the change to middle school with all its new academic opportunities. However, some weeks into the new term Vera learned that, due to an administrative oversight, the middle school received his honors math class recommendation late, and he ended up in a regular class.

In the meantime, Peter's math grades had started to slip. While he had gotten straight As in fourth grade, he was now getting Cs. Aware that bright kids do poorly when they're not challenged, Vera and Tim were convinced he was in the wrong class, and requested that he be moved to the higher level. His teacher wouldn't help—she was convinced his grades were a reflection of his abilities. His guidance counselor wouldn't help—she deferred to the teacher. The vice-principal wouldn't help—it wasn't his area of responsibility. And they each pointed to the next guy as the one who made these decisions.

By this time it was December. Peter's earlier enthusiasm for math was fading fast as he continued to bring home poor grades and question his math smarts. Here was a kid whose favorite subject had been math, whose fourth-grade teacher had raved about his natural gifts and recommended him for the higher class. Vera and Tim finally went directly to the principal and demanded he be moved. She and Tim followed up with daily calls and letters while the administration deliberated.

At last—and Vera believes it was because the staff were tired of resisting their persistent efforts—Peter was allowed to join the high math group right after Christmas vacation. His grade that quarter was an A, and he's gotten straight As on the math fast track right through eleventh grade. This year he's taking honors calculus, honors physics, and honors chemistry—all because his parents stood up for what they believed was best for him back in fifth grade.

You know your children better than anyone else. It's up to you to push for what you believe is right for them. Follow your instincts, and speak up. Whether your children are victims of administrative errors, have to suffer a ruthless or incompetent teacher, stand wrongly accused of something they didn't do, take the fall for a friend, or simply get lost in school because they don't draw attention to themselves—you've got to take a firm stance and correct the situation. You're the only one who can do it for them. Show your kids that problems can be solved, that persistence pays off, and that you'll fight for them until you get results.

One caveat: You have to have the facts right and the evidence to back them up before you take action. It's not enough to hope that your child should be in the gifted program—you have to have test scores, teacher recommendations, and other solid evidence to support your position. And that goes for whatever issue you decide to tackle.

Twelve

AFTER-SCHOOL AND
LEISURE-TIME ACTIVITIES

76.

Keep a Family Calendar

IT'S HARD TO KEEP LIFE SIMPLE while trying to juggle dozens of appointments and commitments, especially when your children are involved in activities outside the home—sports, plays, orthodontics, birthday parties, play dates, and lessons of all kinds. And one universal truth about parenting is that if you don't write it down, you'll forget it.

So keep a large month-by-month calendar in a central location accessible to all family members. The ideal spot is the kitchen counter next to the phone, since most of your appointments are made or canceled by phone.

On the first of each month take a few minutes with your kids to write in their activities for the month—music lessons, scout meetings, hockey practice, and any other things they may have committed to but forgot to mention to you. If you sign up for activities that cover a period of months, enter each activity on your calendar. If you keep a work-related appointment book, be sure to coordinate activities from the family calendar with your personal appointment schedule as needed.

Then, as flyers from school arrive, birthday invitations are accepted, doctor's appointments are made, or soccer games get scheduled, immediately make appropriate entries on the calendar and toss out the notices. Not only will this help you avoid conflicts in scheduling, but if you list the time, address, name, and phone number for each event, you won't have to save the invitation or go digging through miscellaneous scraps of paper and torn envelopes when you have to cancel or postpone.

My friend Emma, who has five children, uses a different colored pen for each of her children. This is not as impossible as it sounds. Keep the pens or a sharpened pencil in a nearby drawer, or in a ceramic mug on the counter, and make it a house rule that no one can remove a pen except to make an entry on the calendar. Not immediately returning the pen to the drawer is a capital offense, punishable by one week of hard labor!

Or consider using a mounted pen holder with a stretch cord attached to the pen, available at hardware or stationery stores, so you always have a writing tool available. Or do what my mother did for years: tie a pencil to a hook on the phone table.

Use the calendar not only as a way to keep track of what each member of the family will be doing at a particular time, but also as a way to make certain you're not overdoing. A calendar bursting at the seams with appointments and activities is a clear sign that you're all doing too much.

At the same time you schedule your kids' regular commitments, schedule some quiet time each week for each child. It's important to actually write quiet time into the schedule so you and your child can count on it, and so other activities don't take over that time. Teach your kids that quiet time is just as important as any other activity they're involved in (#81).

The first of the month is also a good time to look realistically at what you have scheduled, and to *think it through*. Is is actually possible for you to take your son to the dentist to get fitted for braces on the same afternoon you've agreed to host your daughter's scout meeting?

Don't schedule early appointments that will disrupt your family's morning routine or that you'll have to hustle to get to.

If at all possible, schedule appointments and activities so you have to drive only one or two days a week. On the days you drive, arrange your appointments so you have to go out only once that day.

Teach your children to check the calendar before they commit themselves to an activity you may not be able to get them to, or that's at a time they already have something scheduled. And get them started entering their own commitments on the calendar as soon as they can do so legibly.

Get into the habit of looking at the family calendar first thing in the morning, so you'll know what that day's obligations are. If you skip this step, the most diligently updated calendar in the world won't do you any good. Also, be sure to check the calendar at the end of the day so you'll have a chance to organize anything you might need to have ready for the next day.

77.

Don't Overschedule

I TALK TO MANY PARENTS whose lives are unbelievably complicated because their kids are involved in so many different things. The parents know their kids are doing too much, but they feel an obligation—and the social pressure because everyone else is doing it—to expose their kids to as much as possible.

Make life easier for yourself and your kids. They don't need to learn everything now—they have the rest of their lives to explore their interests. Frenetic activity seldom benefits anyone, and they run the risk of burning out early and losing interest in the very activities you hoped they'd pursue.

Think about the skills you want your children to have, and watch to see which activities they really enjoy. Your kids probably already have certain interests, and it's good to develop these early inclinations. Kids learn much better when the passion is their own, not the result of parental pressure.

Limit your kids' activities to one or two per week per season. This way they can enjoy seasonal sports and other activities, and still have time for a game of freeze tag or hide-and-seek with the neighbor kids. Don't let your kids miss out on time for contemplation, reading, thinking, and just plain resting.

As your children get older, they'll eliminate activities that don't hold their interest and stay with those that do. Limiting their activities is a great way to teach your kids that they don't have to do it all.

78.

Get Your Kids Involved in Sports

SPORTS PROVIDE NOURISHMENT for the soul as well as for the body. Kids who are involved in sports tend to be more health-conscious and are far less likely to get into trouble with alcohol, drugs, and delinquent behavior.

Sports also relieve stress and take the focus off home, school, and social problems. A child can't obsess about personal issues while trying to slam-dunk a ball through the hoop, or doing a double somersault off the high board.

Sports teach valuable skills such as discipline, hard work, concentration, team playing, and cooperation, as well as how to be a gracious winner and a good loser. Intimate friendships evolve out of shared team experiences. These are lessons that often can't be learned elsewhere.

As long as you don't get carried away with the number of activities, getting your kids involved in sports can add to the quality of life for all of you.

Some kids seek out competitive sports, others avoid them. If competing turns them off, consider sports such as hiking or kayaking, where there's no score and no finish line. Expose your children to various options. Take them to local games or watch a variety of sports activities on television together to find one they love. Try to find a sport for each season, so they don't have a lot of down time in front of the TV, the computer, or at the video arcade.

Don't get discouraged if your child doesn't respond favorably to the first sports opportunities you introduce her to. Keep trying. There are lots of possibilities.

Not only do sports build a healthy mind and body, but they can pay off in terms of full or partial scholarships. If your child can take advantage of an athletic scholarship, it will greatly simplify your financial life.

If you attend your kids' sports events to cheer them on, keep it simple, for everyone's sake. Don't get carried away by your enthusiasm: refrain from aggressive, overly competitive, raucous demonstrations of support for your child or her team; don't say anything to disparage the opposing team. And never interfere with the referee, umpire, or coach. Remember, you and your kids are involved in sports primarily for the fun of it. And good sportsmanship is still a virtue, no matter what some may say.

79.

Ease Your Driving Load

MENTION AFTER-SCHOOL ACTIVITIES to most parents and their eyes glaze over. One parent or the other, and sometimes both, often spend the hours between the end of school and dinnertime behind the wheel of a car, breathlessly going back and forth to dance classes, swimming lessons, soccer practice, and a score of other activities.

Limiting your kids' activities to one or two per week per child will certainly help ease your driving load. To make things easier still, whenever possible, arrange your children's schedules so they can go straight from school.

When you schedule an activity, make sure you allow enough time to get there and back without having to break speed records. If you find yourself pressed for time, consider dropping an activity. Or switch to one that makes more sense logistically.

When you sign your child up for an activity, get a class list to see who lives nearby that you can carpool with. Take turns with other parents in dropping off and picking up. The more parents there are in the car pool, the less you have to drive.

Research railroad, bus, and subway schedules to see if there's public transportation that will lighten your driving load. And check to see if there's a special student fare.

Make arrangements for your kids to go to a neighbor's or a friend's house if you'll be out when they come home from school. This way you won't be worrying about them, or feeling the need to cut short what you're doing and rush back home to check on them.

If necessary, ask a friend or a neighborhood teenager to help with transportation. If you have a teenager at home who drives, enlist his help in chauffeuring his siblings around. Arrange for your spouse to pick up a child on the way home from work if the time coincides.

If you're the chauffeur, schedule a simple errand while you're waiting for your child to finish—but only if you can do so without having to rush or worry about getting back on time. Better yet, allow yourself to simply sit quietly, breathe deeply, and do nothing for those few precious moments. You've earned it.

Before you return home, use your car phone to make sure your other kids are home or that they have a ride. Then you can go home knowing you won't be called out again the moment you walk in the door.

If you're still feeling overwhelmed with your driving responsibilities, it's time to go back to your family calendar and cut back on the number of activities you and your kids are involved in.

80.

Teach Your Kids to Volunteer

WHEN YOU CONSIDER the types of activities you want your children to be involved in, keep volunteer projects in mind. Children by their very nature live self-centered lives. You want to expand their world beyond their own needs—otherwise demanding and selfish children grow up to be demanding and selfish adults.

Start by teaching your kids to think of others by baby-sitting a neighbor's child, offering to help Grandma walk her dog, taking a warm meal to a sick neighbor, or offering to shovel snow for an elderly friend. Explain that these are neither chores nor paid jobs, but simple gifts from the heart.

Your children will feel a sense of satisfaction and importance as they learn to contribute to the family and the neighborhood.

They can reach out even farther by giving away toys they've outgrown, helping sort things for Goodwill, washing cars for the local swim team fund-raiser, or collecting for the community food drive.

As they get older they can volunteer at a soup kitchen or a museum, help tutor children younger than themselves, or drive a senior citizen to the grocery store. Churches and other religious organizations offer opportunities to volunteer at home and abroad, as do groups like Habitat for Humanity, AmeriCares, and the Red Cross. Or explore the possibility of working for environmental groups that monitor clean water or count whale migrations, or any other endeavors that benefit the planet. Help them find a volunteer job they enjoy and that ties into their interests.

As your kids learn to look beyond their own needs to those of others, not only does your job get easier, but you'll be raising responsible citizens who will continue to contribute not only to the family, but to the entire community.

81.

Encourage Quiet Time

ALL OF US, YOUNG AND OLD, need time to get in touch with our feelings—catch our breath, review the past, contemplate the present, and make plans for the future. And everyone can benefit from peace and quiet, simply because it's peaceful and quiet.

Teach your children to appreciate solitude, to derive simple pleasure from a beach walk, a mountain hike, or a good book. As you limit their use of TV, video games, and the phone, they'll stop needing the stimulation of electronic media and learn to rely on their own inner resources.

Teach them about the wonders of nature. Point out the special beauty of a thunderstorm, or weather of any type. Never pass up an opportunity to let them romp in the rain, collect hail, play in the snow, chase butterflies, turn cartwheels on the lawn, or lie under the shade of a tree.

Point out beautiful sunsets, the first forsythia blooms in early spring, a laundry line draped with colorful quilts, horses grazing in a pasture, or the simple beauty of a clear blue sky at noon.

And give them the opportunity to show you what they observe.

You'll see things you've never seen before—a stick shaped like a rocket ship, a wriggling worm under a rock, a cloud formation that looks like Mickey Mouse.

Give your kids the time and encouragement to draw, paint, make music, or take photographs, or simply to sit quietly and day-dream so they become comfortable with silence and their own thoughts.

What better gift to give your children than a rich inner life, a strong sense of self-reliance, and an appreciation for the world around them?

Thirteen

OUTINGS AND TRAVEL

82.

Keep Your Car Battle-Ready

SOMETIMES EVEN A SHORT TRIP into town for milk is a challenge for kids who are tired or hungry. Make your car as user-friendly as possible so you and your kids can survive any trip, and especially those that end up being longer than you anticipated.

Get a couple of boxes, or any other easily stored containers with tight lids.

In one, the provisions container, keep:

A supply of healthy snacks, such as popcorn or dried fruit.

A supply of drinking water.

Chewable Dramamine tablets for kids who are prone to car sickness.

Envelopes of moist towelettes for messy hands and faces

Paper napkins, tissues, half a dozen paper towels.

In the other, the entertainment container, keep:

A couple of children's books.

Some favorite toys.

Markers and a sketch pad.

Teach your kids to return these things to the entertainment box when they've finished with them or at the end of each trip, whichever comes first.

It's also helpful to have a third container, for supplies to help you with mishaps and emergencies. These might include:

A box of small adhesive bandages.

A roll of paper towels for cleaning up inevitable messes.

Spray cleaners for windows and for cleaning spills on car upholstery.

A throw-up container—you never know when the kids will need one.

A flashlight with a strobe feature for breakdowns.

Keep these containers accessible. Inspect them from time to time to be sure nothing has spilled or been used up, and that the batteries are charged and ready.

Keep a good-sized trash container in your car and teach your kids to use it. You can stow extra trash bags in the emergency cleanup box.

In the glove compartment or a nearby seat pocket keep a local map. Also keep an address book with telephone numbers of your kids' friends, their schools, and any other places they might be waiting when you're running late and need to let them know.

You'll find your car trips are simpler and more pleasant when you have the means at hand to feed and water your kids, while keeping them happily occupied.

83.

Who Gets to Sit in the Front?

YOU'VE NO DOUBT had to deal with fights between siblings over who gets to sit where on a car trip. The front passenger seat is the highly coveted prize. Winning that seat is a symbol of power and supremacy over those who've lost out and are forced to ride in the back. If you have more than one child, you've no doubt had to deal with this contest of wills. Whether the trip you're embarking on is a cross-country trek or a two-minute hop to the local deli, the competition can be fierce.

If your car has a front passenger seat air bag, don't let a small child sit there. Children and small adults (under 120 pounds) have been seriously injured or killed by these air bags.

Otherwise a simple solution is to assign each child his own back seat space in the car. Then let the kids decide which one of them gets to sit in the front, for how long, and who goes first. If they can't decide or if an argument ensues, put them all in their assigned back seats until they can peacefully negotiate their turns up front.

You might be surprised at how quickly your children will stop arguing over the front seat, and how easily they'll work together to figure out what's fair. You may find they'll each still try to sneak an extra turn every now and then, but when they're called on it by their siblings they tend to give up without a fight, because they know if they do fight, no one gets the front seat.

The best part is that you no longer have to arbitrate the battles, except occasionally. When the kids can't come to terms on their own, it's simple—they all get exiled to the back of the car.

84.

Clarify Your Expectations

OFTEN YOUR CHILDREN let you down when you're on an outing, and you end up feeling disappointed or even embarrassed by their behavior. All you want is their cooperation—is that too much to ask? Well, actually, sometimes it is, especially when you haven't let them know what you expect of them.

So before you leave, or on your way to your destination, let your kids know exactly how you want them to behave. If you're going to a friend's house, remind them of their manners—to make eye contact when they're saying hello, and to say please and thank-you when appropriate. Also let them know what behaviors won't be tolerated—no fighting, no tantrums, no wild shoot-'em-up games.

If you can avoid it, don't take your kids out when you know they're tired or hungry, or when they aren't feeling well and are likely to create a scene. Most outings aren't emergencies, so wait until everyone is in a more positive frame of mind.

If you simply must go out at times like this, make it quick, and come home as soon as possible. Or take advantage of delivery services, car pools, baby-sitters, your driving-age teens, or an otherwise unoccupied spouse.

When you embark on an excursion, let your kids know what they're in for. Tell them where you're going, who you'll be seeing, what you'll be doing, and how long you'll be staying.

Keep your word. It's not fair for you to expect your kids, especially older kids who may have plans of their own, to go along quietly with a sudden change of plan such as your desire to stay at a gathering longer than you said you would because you're in the middle of what to you is a fascinating conversation. Sometimes a change will agree with your children; other times it won't. You have to respect their wants and needs if you want their cooperation.

Don't push your luck. When you're in the middle of a wonderful meal at a nice restaurant with your mate and your kids and one of the kids starts to fuss, this isn't the time to order dessert and linger over coffee. Older children can be reasoned with, but when a young child reaches the end of his rope—at a restaurant, in a store, in the middle of a movie—there's not much you can do to turn the situation around. Better to cut your trip short than to have to deal with a fussy, crying, or obstreperous child.

From the time they're very little, praise your kids when they behave well on outings. Tell them how proud you are and how much fun it is to go out with them. This will provide a major incentive for them to behave well on the next outing.

85

Grocery Shopping with Kids

THE KEY TO SIMPLE GROCERY SHOPPING is organization. Plan your meals ahead of time so you can get by with only one trip to the grocery store each week. Well, and maybe a short trip or two when you run out of milk or eggs.

Make up a master list of the items you purchase regularly and run off copies of it to use as your weekly shopping list. Check your stock against this list before you go out shopping. If you arrange the list in the same order that the items appear in the aisles of the supermarket, you never have to backtrack—saving, in the new supermarkets, up to a quarter-mile of walking.

Kids can be either a hindrance or a help to you in the grocery store, so start training them when they're young to be helpful. Call out the next item on your list and make a game of seeing who can find it first. By the time they can read, put them in charge of the pen and the list. Have them call out the next item and check it off the list when you find it.

Children can help load and unload your shopping cart. Or let them have their own cart for picking out their snacks and school lunch supplies. Just make sure you retain veto rights on their choices.

One mother I know has her kids clip coupons and hunt down those items when they go shopping—the kids get to keep the savings. Another friend puts his son in charge of the return cans and bottles to recycle—his son gets to keep the deposit money.

Make sure your child has a snack before you get into the store. If he gets hungry while you're in the store, open your loaf of bread and let him have a slice rather than having him eat sweets or other snacks that might spoil his dinner. My mother always said if we weren't hungry enough to eat a slice of bread, we weren't very hungry.

Never give in to a tantrum. If your child makes a scene in the supermarket, try to calm her down, and once again calmly and clearly outline the consequences if she doesn't shape up. But if you see that she's out of control, abandon your cart where it is and go home, making it clear that next time she won't get to come along.

Leaving the store in the middle of a shopping excursion is certainly an inconvenience, but if you stick to your guns and don't take her with you next time, it's a lesson she won't soon forget. It'll make all future shopping excursions with her easier.

Of course, the simplest way to grocery shop is to have a list and go alone. This saves a lot of time and energy and eliminates having to wrestle with coats, hats, boots, gloves, car seats, and seat belts.

Supermarkets have expanded in recent years to include everything from dry cleaning to photo processing. Take advantage of these services to cut down on extra stops, which take time and energy and are an extra strain on you and your kids.

86.

Make Eating Out a Pleasant Experience

IT'S AMAZING HOW ENJOYABLE a restaurant meal can be without children, and what a nightmare it can often turn into when kids come along. Arguments about where to sit, sibling spats, spilled drinks, raised voices, and wasted food can make eating out something to avoid instead of a treat to look forward to.

Remember that dining out is a skill your kids have to be taught, just like any other skill. You can't expect a youngster to behave perfectly on his first visit to a restaurant any more than you'd expect him to know how to play tennis without knowing the rules of the game.

Here are some things to keep in mind the next time you go out to eat with the kids:

Make it easy on yourself by choosing a restaurant that caters to children—like restaurants that have paper tablecloths and a box of crayons on the table for the kids.

If you're trying out a new restaurant, make sure the kids know what kind of food will be served and roughly how long it will take. There are few things more frustrating than trying to convince a child he'll like spinach quiche when he has his taste buds set for hamburger and fries.

Again, let your children know that misbehavior will not be tolerated. Explain the consequences if they act up. For example, at the first sign of trouble, you'll all leave the restaurant; no one will get dessert; the problem child will wait in the car while the rest of you finish—assuming he's old enough to be alone in the car; or he won't get to go next time. These are good logical consequences.

If you have kids who are not getting along with each other at the moment, don't seat them next to each other. Put a parent or a cooperative child between the two to keep peace.

Bring drawing pens and paper, a book, or small toys with you to keep your kids quietly amused while you wait for the food to arrive. (Doing this for any outing will make waiting with young children easier—from waiting for the dentist to waiting while your tires get rotated.)

Eat as close to your regular family mealtime as possible. You can't expect a child who's used to eating at six P.M. to hold out until eight.

Ask the server to bring a basket of bread or a salad right away so the kids don't get restless while waiting.

If one of the children is a finicky eater, make sure you order something both you and the child like; if he rejects the stuffed cannelloni he promised he'd eat, you can switch meals. Or order an appetizer or a half-portion for yourself if you know your child won't finish his own meal.

As always, retain veto rights on your kids' selections, and give them options—they can have the chicken or the fish, but not the spareribs, when you know they won't like the spareribs.

Don't order anything that takes a long time to cook.

As your kids get older and you're more confident that they'll behave themselves, let them sit at a table on their own. It's fun for them, and it can feel like a night out for you at your table for two.

And don't forget to praise your children when they behave well.

87.

Teach Your Kids How to Pack

VERA USED TO DREAD going on overnight trips with her kids because it meant that she had to pack all their stuff as well as her own, and then she'd get blamed when a favorite T-shirt or teddy bear got left behind.

In desperation, she taught her kids to pack for themselves. Andrew's been packing for himself since he was four. Here's how they do it:

Each child gets his own duffel bag, so he can be responsible for his own things before, during, and after the trip.

The kids lay out on their beds everything they think they'll need for the excursion. Vera checks to see if they have enough underwear and socks, and to make sure they haven't forgotten anything important. She also edits their choices so they don't pack more stuff than they need. Then they pack their own bags.

In addition to whatever toiletries they may pack for themselves—shampoo, toothpaste, toothbrush—she takes along a separate kit stocked for everyone. This might include things like a thermometer, adhesive bandages, Dramamine, an aural analgesic for middle-of-the-night earaches, an extra toothbrush, soap, and suntan lotion. She keeps this bag stocked and packed, so it's always ready for the next trip.

On long car trips, the children bring pillows and blankets, plus their own stash of snacks and drinks that they can help themselves to during the ride. They pack the food themselves, too.

You'll want to double-check that the security blanket or the teddy bear was packed. But limit the number of toys, because they're hard to keep track of en route, they get lost easily, and they are seldom played with enough to warrant the space they take. Make the kids responsible for their own toys. If they lose one, it's a valuable lesson—they'll be more careful next time.

88.

Make Traveling Fun

EVEN THOUGH TRAVELING with kids can add a whole new level of complexity to being on the road, it also offers unparalleled opportunities for shared experiences that can enrich your lives forever. My friend Jeanne believes traveling is much more fun with her four kids than without them. She and her husband get to see the world with the wonder, delight, and sense of discovery her children bring to each new place.

Both my husband, Gibbs, and Vera's husband, Tim, are travel writers. Consequently we've all traveled thousands of miles around the world with our kids. It's not always simple, but we've learned there are some things you can do to make traveling with kids easier.

Since part of the fun of traveling is in the planning, be sure to involve your children in this stage of a trip, keeping your budget and time constraints in mind. And by including the kids in the planning you greatly reduce the chances of bringing along a child who is bored or doesn't want to be there, and can make the trip miserable for everyone else.

Don't open the discussion by asking what they'd like to do on their next vacation—unless you're prepared to spring for an African safari. Instead, give them options. Ask whether they'd rather go to the beach or the mountains, skiing or swimming, Disney World or Club Med. Then work within your circumstances to design a trip everyone will enjoy.

Avoid overly ambitious itineraries. Trying to visit seven cities in five days won't be easy or fun for anyone.

Keep the weather and local conditions in mind when planning a trip. You don't want to be arriving at the height of the rainy season, when temperatures are extreme, or when mosquitoes the size of golf balls are out in full force.

Older kids usually entertain themselves on a long journey, but be prepared to keep your younger kids amused and interested. If you're visiting a part of the country or the world they've never been to before, keep a map handy so you can discuss your destination. Talk about what you'll be doing, the activities that will be available, and some of the experiences they'll be likely to encounter.

Bring along simple snack food, a book or two, and a pad and drawing supplies. Play games like twenty questions, the license-plate game if you're on the road (make a list of the state license plates you see, trying to find all fifty states), and other travel games. Sing songs, listen to music or books-on-tape, read aloud to each other, or tell stories. And be sure to point out the particular beauty of any landscape, even seemingly boring ones.

Book your reservations and seat assignments well in advance if you're traveling by plane, otherwise you may have a problem getting seated together.

I've tried every trick in the book and have found there are a couple of things you can do to greatly minimize jet lag for all of you. First, as much as possible, plan your flight so you don't arrive in the dark, or late at night, when the kids will be tired and cranky.

Second, approach jet lag as a mind-over-matter issue. When you fasten your seat belt, set your watch to the time it currently is at your destination and, for the rest of your trip, forget about what time it is back home. Encourage your kids to nap on the plane, and keep their snacks handy for nourishment. Then, when you land, avoid the temptation to "rest up from your flight." Get going, and soak up as much sunshine and fresh air as you can. Go to bed and have your meals at your normal time in the time zone where you now are.

Third, and perhaps most importantly, stay hydrated. Before, during, and after your flight drink six to eight glasses of water a day. Encourage your kids to drink as much as they can. This will result in more trips to the bathroom, but the trade-off in terms of how they feel will be worth it. Carry water in an over-the-shoulder sling bag and fill up as needed. Being hydrated makes a tremendous difference in your body's reaction to the rigors of being on the road.

Be flexible. If you find that you're doing too much, the hotel isn't just right, or the road is washed out, be prepared to move on to some place new. Or if you find an ideal spot, hear of an interesting side trip, or want to explore an area a bit longer than you had anticipated, be prepared to modify your plans. Leave room in your itinerary for spontaneity and you'll all have a lot more fun.

Most importantly, make sure you and your kids are psychologically prepared for anything—missed connections, bad weather, inoperable gear, or whatever else might not go as you expected. Sometimes a forced change of plans can be more exciting and more memorable than your original plan could ever have been. With the right attitude, you can make an adventure out of anything, and teach your kids to do the same.

Fourteen
HEALTH

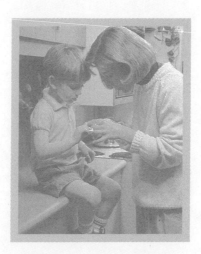

89.

Find a Doctor You Like

YOUR RELATIONSHIP with your pediatrician begins the moment the doctor examines your newborn for the first time. From then on, your pediatrician will see you when things are good—for routine monthly or yearly physicals. And he or she will also be the one you turn to when you and your children are the most vulnerable—when your kids are sick.

It's vitally important that you choose the right doctor for your family. This is the person to whom you've entrusted the health and welfare of your children. It's imperative that your pediatrician be not just medically competent but emotionally supportive.

Ask other parents for recommendations when you're selecting a pediatrician. Often you'll hear the same name over and over again. Interview that doctor, and perhaps several others. Check their credentials.

One of the most important factors in choosing a pediatrician is that you find someone you can easily and openly communicate with. You should feel free to ask questions, no matter how trivial they may seem, without feeling stupid or rushed. Good pediatricians understand that parents can be nervous when it comes to their kids' health, and will go out of their way to reassure them and answer whatever questions they have.

The pediatrician you choose should:

Be personable and accessible.

Be someone your children like and feel comfortable with.

Speak directly to your kids and reassure them during visits.

Not keep you waiting for your scheduled appointment. Office waits of longer than twenty minutes, except in cases of emergencies, should be brought to the attention of the doctor. This may be a front office problem that the doctor isn't aware of and will want to correct.

Be immediately available in case of an emergency, or have another doctor covering who will take care of your child right away.

Call you back within an hour if your child is very sick. If you don't get a return call immediately, keep calling until you reach the doctor or someone who can address your concerns. If the situation is not urgent, give the doctor until the end of the workday to respond.

Be able to recognize signs of emotional or mental distress. Your children's yearly physicals should always include a friendly conversation with the doctor on how things are going. A good pediatrician pays particular attention to the manner in which the children answer, as well as listening carefully to what they have to say.

Remember that this relationship is in one respect like any other—it takes two to make it work. Communicate your concerns, ask questions, tell your doctor when you're not happy and why, resolve differences, and work together for the benefit of your kids. Directly address issues that make you uncomfortable, and if you're still not satisfied after discussing your concerns, change doctors.

When you have the right pediatrician—and you're confident that you have someone knowledgeable and supportive to turn to when you're concerned about your children's health or behavior—every other aspect of parenting becomes much simpler.

90.

Teach Your Kids to Eat Right and Be Healthy

IT IS MUCH SIMPLER to keep a child healthy than it is to treat an ailing one.

A well-balanced diet and lots of exercise are vitally important to your children's overall health. Keep snacks of fruit and vegetables within easy reach. One reader said her kids always knew where to find healthy snacks. As soon as they were able to open the fridge by themselves, she started keeping chopped veggies in a container on the bottom shelf.

Don't buy junk food, and be very selective about the types of food you have in the house. Be sure to set a good example. If junk food is readily available to them, and if they see you constantly munching on candy and chips and drinking sodas, they'll want to do the same. This greatly increases the possibility that they'll grow up to be overweight adults with a variety of health problems.

Consider your children's nutritional requirements, but don't worry if they occasionally go on a strange eating binge where they eat only one thing three times a day for three weeks. For instance, between the age of one and a half and age five or six, a child may decide she won't eat any colored foods. Pediatricians call this the "white diet." Pasta, white bread, milk, cheese or grilled cheese, turkey, chicken, apples (pared of their noxiously colored red or green skins, of course), bananas, pancakes, waffles—sometimes hard-boiled or scrambled eggs—are all acceptable to kids on this diet. For reasons that defy logic, they are not as adversely affected by the colors of chocolate and other candy.

These phases can last from a few weeks to several months. If you have a child going through such a stage, experiment by offering her a piece of juicy watermelon, a strawberry, or a grape. Eventually she'll come around and add other foods to her diet. Look at the whole week, rather than the daily intake, to make sure your kids are getting the vitamins and minerals they need.

Preventive medicine also includes making sure your kids get regular physicals and vaccinations as well as yearly eye exams and dental checkups. It means avoiding or minimizing tooth decay and gum disease by teaching them to brush their teeth carefully at least twice a day and showing them—or making sure their dentist shows them—how to floss correctly once their permanent teeth are in. It means teaching them that loud noises such as high-volume radios, stereos, and tape players can seriously damage their hearing—much more quickly than they might think. And it means making certain their shoes fit properly so they don't develop foot problems.

Get your kids in the habit of taking good care of their bodies while they're young, and they'll grow up to be physically fit adults.

91.

Follow Basic Safety Rules

PREVENTING ACCIDENTS is easier than dealing with a hurt child. You need to minimize the risks your children will encounter and, as they get older, teach them about situations that could be dangerous and how to avoid them.

If you've ever watched a toddler eat sand, drink the contents of a medicine bottle, or chase the cat into the middle of the road, you know how important it is to provide constant supervision and firm reminders about what's safe and what isn't.

You can't turn your back for one second. That's enough time for a young child to make a break for the road, fall down the steps, or knock boiling water off the stove. Vigilance is essential—as is patience. The toddler years are the most trying age for parents. Be sure you get a break regularly (#8) so you can stay alert and focused.

Here are some guidelines:

When your child is a baby, be sure to use car seats, cribs, and other equipment that meets government safety standards. Use approved car seats designed for your child's age and weight. Have your kids ride in their car seats in the back seat until they're big enough to use a standard seat belt. Front passenger-seat airbags can seriously injure or even kill small children. If you have a passenger-side airbag, put young kids in the back seat.

When your kids are just beginning to crawl, they become much more vulnerable to injury. Use stairway gates and window guards where appropriate. Childproof the house by getting down on your hands and knees for a child's-eye perspective of the potential dangers in your home. Lock cabinets, move houseplants, shut doors, cover electrical outlets, put dangerous objects out of reach, and watch your adventurous child every second of his waking day to make certain he survives this daredevil age.

Make sure all medicines and cleaning solvents are locked away.

Keep your kids away from stoves—especially the ones with flat cooking surfaces that make it difficult to tell when they're turned on.

Teach your children to swim. Point out the shallow and deep areas of the pool or beach. Warn them about currents and cramps, and make sure they know what to do in an emergency. Never let your children swim alone, and teach them to respect the water. The daughter of a friend of mine lost two friends who went boating in the middle of winter unaware of the dangers of hypothermia. The boat capsized, and they died within a few yards of shore.

Use whatever safety gear is available for the sports your children are involved in—helmets for football, riding, and biking;

knee, elbow, and wrist pads for rollerblading; life preservers for boating, and so on.

Teach your kids the rules of the road, whether walking or biking.

Make sure your kids know what to do if strangers, or friends or relatives, suggest something inappropriate or dangerous—especially when it concerns alcohol, drugs, or sexual misconduct.

Teach your children to tell you if anything inappropriate or hurtful has happened to them—especially if they've been threatened not to talk. Prepare yourself to respond calmly so they won't be further traumatized by your reaction.

Help your children develop strategies to resist peer pressure. They need to learn how to excuse themselves from anyone engaged in reckless behavior, whether it's drugs, drinking, gunplay, fireworks, vandalism, or drag racing. Role-play with them so they'll know how to get out of these and other dangerous situations. Make sure your kids know you'll come and pick them up, no questions asked, if they find themselves in a dangerous situation.

Car accidents are a high-risk factor in the lives of teenagers. Driving while under the influence, joyriding, a disregard for the rules of the road and the rights of other drivers all too frequently lead to critical injuries or fatalities among teens. Teach your child how to drive safely. Car privileges are a reward for mature and responsible behavior, and should be revoked if your child shows he's not ready for this responsibility. His life is at stake—this is no time for leniency.

Through their own experience and your guidance, toddlers eventually grow into children with common sense. By the time they're three, they can be left alone for a brief time to play indoors by themselves as long as you're nearby to supervise. As kids get older, they do get smarter. But never for a moment take it for granted that your children will be able to handle a situation safely unless you've discussed it with them beforehand. Whether it's diving into the wrong end of the pool, taking a ride with strangers, or biking without a helmet, life can be risky for kids who haven't learned basic safety rules.

92.

Common Ailments to Be Aware Of

MOST CHILDREN'S AILMENTS are the result of a nasty bug that's going around—conditions that time alone heals. But when it's the middle of the night and your child is suffering, you want to be able to alleviate the discomfort and pain.

There are home remedies and over-the-counter remedies that can help you through some of the common ailments you're likely to encounter with your kids. Here, and in the rest of this chapter, are some things Vera has learned from working with her pediatrician, Dr. Norman Weinberger, over the past seventeen years. Before you administer any medication, be sure to check with your pediatrician so you know exactly what you're treating. And *never* give medications of any kind to an infant unless instructed to by your doctor.

Colds and flus. There's little you can do except make your child more comfortable. Be sure she gets plenty of rest. Most doctors recommend acetaminophen or ibuprofen to bring a fever down. Though allowing a *low-grade* fever to run its course may actually be beneficial, since an elevated temperature is one of the body's ways of fighting infection. Have her drink lots of fluids.

Stomach viruses. Let your child's digestive system rest for a while before giving her anything to eat or drink, then start with small amounts of clear liquids, popsicles, Jell-O, and the like. Follow with a bland diet for the next twenty-four hours. Avoid milk products, fatty foods, and roughage. If your child can't keep anything down, be careful she doesn't get dehydrated. Having her suck on ice cubes or popsicles helps. Keep some Pedialyte on hand to provide nutrients.

Sore throats. Have your child gargle with warm water and salt. See the doctor to rule out strep.

Croup. Croup is the name given to a distinctive cough that comes from an infection of the voice box. Most parents aren't prepared for their first case of croup. Vera had never heard of it until one night she was startled by a cough that sounded like the bark of a distressed seal. She was shocked to find Peter gasping for breath and panicked by his own condition.

Don't be frightened by the sound of the cough or the quickened breathing and sucking for air that accompany croup. It's relatively easy to treat. You can make a steam room out of your bathroom by running a hot tub or shower and letting your child sit in the room until his breathing eases. If that doesn't work, wrap him warmly and take him out into the cold night air for a few minutes. If that still doesn't work, call the doctor or go to the nearest emergency room. Most importantly, relax—it sounds much worse than it is.

Ear pain. Most kids don't notice an earache until they go to sleep and are awakened by the pain in their ear. It's not an emergency, but you still want to make your child comfortable. You can use ear drops, such as Auralgan, to relieve the pain. The drops are applied directly into the sore ear. Putting a heating pad on the ear may help, as may laying the child on the other ear so the sore ear drains. Make an appointment to see the doctor the following day.

Growth pains. Lots of kids complain of joint pain when they're going through growth spurts. But it's also a symptom of Lyme disease as well as other serious illnesses. Reduce the pain with painkillers or heating pads, but if it persists beyond a few days, or if you have any doubts about the reason for the pain, call the doctor.

Skin problems. There are so many conditions with dermatological symptoms that you have to assess each case individually. Have your pediatrician look for an underlying cause like an allergy, a viral infection, Lyme disease, chicken pox, heat rash, insect bites, or poison ivy. You can get some comfort from the itching of the rash itself with Benadryl, which is available as either a topical ointment or oral syrup. An oatmeal bath can help reduce the itching from a bad case of chicken pox.

93.

Remedies, Potions, and Supplies to Keep on Hand

IT'S MIDNIGHT and your child is running a fever and crying because every time she lies down her ear hurts. What do you do?

Many painful symptoms of otherwise common illnesses can be alleviated with remedies you can keep at home for just such emergencies. Though regulations may vary from state to state, most of the items listed here can be purchased over the counter. Check with your pediatrician first, but here are some things you might want to have on hand:

Painkillers. For relief of pain and fever reduction, your doctor will probably recommend acetaminophen or ibuprofen—both are effective. Never give children aspirin—the combination of aspirin and viral illness dramatically increases the risk of a very serious illness called Reyes Syndrome.

Acetaminophen suppositories. Can help reduce a fever when a child has been vomiting and can't keep anything down.

Decongestants. They work on some kids and not on others—some make kids hyper, others make them drowsy. Ask your pediatrician for advice. If you use a decongestant, be sure to read the directions carefully first.

Saline nose sprays. These are a suitable lubricant for dry, crusty noses and can be used on kids of any age.

Ear drops. Auralgan is an analgesic that will numb the pain of an earache and make it easier for your child to sleep. These drops will not heal the underlying infection, so call the doctor the next day— even if your child seems to feel better.

Benadryl. An antihistamine given to alleviate the symptoms of allergy, Benadryl is also useful in some kids as a decongestant. It also helps when you are at your wit's end with children who can't sleep because of nose stuffiness or ear pain.

Betadine. An antiseptic liquid to be applied to a wound after it's been thoroughly cleaned with soap and water.

Bacitracin. A topical ointment for preventing infection and clearing up some rashes.

Lotrimin. An anti-fungicide cream that's a godsend for athlete's foot and some stubborn diaper rashes. Consult your doctor first to make sure it's a fungal infection you're treating.

Benadryl cream. A topical cream used to alleviate itching from rashes or bug bites.

Pedialyte, Gatorade, Powerade, and the like. Energy drinks packed with electrolytes for a child who has lost a lot of fluids through vomiting or diarrhea. They replace many essential nutrients and help your child on the road to recovery.

Syrup of ipecac induces vomiting in case of poisoning. But be aware that some poisons burn on the way down, and you'll do further damage if you force vomiting with these. Call the poison control center before taking any action.

Adhesive bandages of all shapes and sizes, plus gauze pads and first-aid tape.

Be sure you have a thermometer. An old-fashioned mercury-tipped glass thermometer is the best. A digital thermometer is convenient but not nearly as accurate. A rectal temperature is the most accurate because other factors can influence temperatures taken orally or under the arm.

That said, I've talked with many parents who've never taken their children's temperature rectally. It's much easier to take a temperature orally, and it can be just as accurate as a rectal temperature, though an oral temperature reads one degree less than a rectal temperature; an under-the-arm temperature reads two degrees less. You can take a baby's temperature under the arm while nursing or giving her a bottle.

Be sure to keep all medications out of reach of small children who may mistakenly believe that they're candies. And be careful to never put that idea into a child's head by telling him that the medicine you're trying to get him to take tastes like candy.

Read the labels of all medicines very carefully and follow the directions for your child's age and weight. And be sure to keep in touch with your pediatrician regarding updated findings and changes in recommended remedies and appropriate doses.

Call the doctor if you have any questions.

94.

Know When to Call the Doctor

CALL THE DOCTOR whenever you have a question about your child's health. Your concern is sufficient reason to phone. You know your child better than anyone does, so you're the best judge of determining when something is wrong—physically or behaviorally. Trust your instincts.

Don't worry about "bothering" the doctor. That's what he or she is there for. If your concern is minor, the nurse or nurse-practitioner can probably help you. For more serious matters, insist on speaking to the doctor.

The following are symptoms that should always be taken seriously:

Earaches. Kids, especially children under five, get lots of ear infections. Babies, who can't yet tell you what hurts, may pull at their ears, be irritable, and have trouble sleeping. When they're lying down, fluid doesn't drain as easily, and the resulting pressure causes extreme pain. Decreased appetite may also be a sign of an ear infection.

Sore throats. If you're sure your child's sore throat isn't due to postnasal drip, then you have to get a throat culture to rule out strep throat. Untreated strep can lead to heart disease.

Eye trouble. Conjunctivitis will cause the white of the eye to be bloodshot and pus will form in the eye. Sometimes a child awakening with conjunctivitis will find that his eyes are glued shut. Most eye problems should be checked by the doctor. Eye pain always warrants an examination.

Abdominal pain. Call if you suspect appendicitis. Indications include vomiting, fever, and acute pain in the lower right abdomen.

Severe vomiting or diarrhea. If your child has been vomiting or has very loose and frequent bowel movements, there is a danger of dehydration. Signs include decreased urination, an absence of tears, and very dry mouth and skin. This can become a serious condition if left unattended—an infant can lose as much as 10 percent of his body weight with one bad bout of diarrhea.

General distress. Difficulty in breathing or pain that doesn't go away. Any kind of acute distress should be quickly attended to by a doctor.

The unexplainable. If your child shows no other symptoms but is suddenly lethargic, hyperactive, or clumsy, and you find yourself worrying about odd behavior, by all means call the doctor. Sometimes a serious illness has subtle symptoms. Behavioral changes are the first signs of depression, substance abuse, eating disorders, or other conditions that need medical attention.

Fever. Fever is defined as a rectal temperature of 100.4 degrees Fahrenheit using a mercury-tipped rectal thermometer. If your child is six months of age or younger or if he has become delirious, he needs to be seen by your pediatrician for a fever. Otherwise, it's the body's natural reaction to fighting infection.

Many parents associate high fever with seizures, but you should know that seizures can happen with a fever as low as 102 degrees F. Seizures are associated with high temperatures as well as with a rapid change in temperature. Your pediatrician will probably tell you that if fever is a child's *only* symptom, she doesn't need to be seen.

Headache. Severe headaches, especially accompanied by stiffness in the neck or a sensitivity to light, are symptoms of meningitis.

Skin rashes. Some rashes come and go in a matter of hours, but others are a sign of illness. Lyme disease, characterized by a bull's-eye rash, can be debilitating if not caught in its early stages. See the doctor for any skin disorders that seem strange to you or last more than three days.

Any symptoms that last for more than four days. Viruses like colds usually last five to ten days. If symptoms persist, complications may develop, and will need to be treated by a doctor.

Get a second opinion or consult with a specialist if you feel you need to. You are your child's greatest health advocate, and the

medical establishment, especially under HMOs, can seem imper-
sonal and bureaucratic. That's because it is. If you've chosen your
pediatrician well, he or she can be of great help in getting your
child the treatment she needs.

95.

Know What to Do for Emergencies

IT IS HELPFUL TO KNOW which conditions need emergency care, what can wait for the doctor the next morning, and what you can do when faced with an emergency. The following need immediate treatment:

Breathing difficulties. Any kind of breathing difficulty needs to be dealt with immediately. Even a child accustomed to suffering a mild form of croup or asthma may experience a much more severe case than usual that necessitates medical intervention. Choking or a severe allergic reaction can also block a child's airway.

Acute pain. Any pain that is beyond what you consider normal, or that doesn't go away, should be seen by a physician immediately.

Bleeding. Profuse bleeding needs to be stopped immediately and then treated. Some deep puncture wounds don't bleed that much, but still require emergency care before more serious problems develop. Signs of blood in a child's saliva, vomit, urine, or stool are an indication of internal bleeding—see a doctor right away.

Accidents. Whenever your child has been in an accident of any kind, he should be evaluated immediately. He may need to be treated for shock, and you have no way of knowing if there's internal damage. For the same reason call the doctor immediately if your child suffers any sort of blunt trauma where there is pain or discomfort but no broken skin, such as a heavy blow to the head or a severe kick in the stomach.

Altered states of consciousness. If your child is unconscious, it's obvious that you need to get help immediately. But consider it an emergency if there's *any* change in your child's level of consciousness. There are critical conditions, such as a drug overdose, alcohol poisoning, and meningitis, among others, that affect a child's consciousness. You are the best judge of your child's varying moods and energy levels—get help when you feel your child is behaving outside the norm.

Ingested poisons. Call your physician and your local poison control center as soon as you discover that your child has consumed anything out of the ordinary. (Keep both numbers on your emergency phone list next to the phone.) Know which household items are poisonous—bleach and ammonia, even some houseplants, among many others.

Your child should be seen by your physician if you suspect she may have ingested too many children's chewable medicine tablets—these can cause liver failure in amounts you'd never suspect to be dangerous. Keep syrup of ipecac, for inducing vomiting, on hand, but again, never use it without direct instructions from a poison control expert.

Burns. Burns should be seen immediately so they can be properly evaluated and treated. Soaking the affected area in ice water will stop the burn from doing further damage, but never apply ice directly to the affected area. Then get medical attention right away—severe burns cannot and should not be treated at home.

Broken bones and sprains should be evaluated and treated by a doctor as soon as possible.

Fire, electric shock, choking, animal and insect bites, and drowning are all accidents that can happen to you and your family. Your first course of action is to be prepared. You, your spouse, and your older children should enroll in an infant and child CPR and first aid course, so you'll know what to do until medical help arrives.

Be sure to have smoke alarms as needed in your home and teach your kids what to do in case of fire. Have a fire drill at home as they do at school. If you have a fire extinguisher, show your kids how to use it. Never let your children play with matches.

Even your youngest child should know how to call 911. You should all know what information to give to 911 when there is an emergency. And keep a list of numbers to call in an emergency by the main telephone, easily accessible to all members of the family.

96.

Consider Alternative Therapies

ACUPUNCTURE, accupressure, massage, homeopathy, chiropractic care, biofeedback, hypnotherapy, hydrotherapy, light and music therapy, vitamin, herbal, and other alternative therapies are becoming more and more popular. Many of these can be effective in delivering relief from various illnesses, aches, and pains. But, because some of these treatments are unregulated and many practitioners are unlicensed, you have to be very careful when choosing them.

Many Western doctors are disdainful of alternative medicines, so you may feel reticent about asking your pediatrician about them. Still, I urge you to consult with your children's doctor before trying anything new. You need to know about the possible dangers, if there are any. Most of the time, the doctor will wish you good luck and send you on your way.

Peter suffered from severe headaches when school first began last year. Standard medicine had nothing to offer him other than pain relievers. Vera took him to a massage therapist, and after a couple of sessions his headaches were gone. They were caused by muscle spasms in his neck and shoulders. Rather than treating his symptoms, massage eliminated the underlying problem.

Get a personal and professional recommendation when choosing a practitioner, and use common sense when dealing with any medical practitioners. Use the same criteria as you do when choosing a pediatrician—check personal references, credentials, training, and experience. Many states require licensing, so make sure any practitioner you use is certified or licensed. Be wary of zealots who believe every ailment can be treated successfully with their form of therapy.

97.

What to Do When Your Child Is Sick

IN THE BEST OF TIMES, getting through the day is a challenge. When your child is ill, the routine you've worked so hard to establish is disrupted. A sick child needs constant attention and care. You must focus on her needs before anything else—a daunting task in families where both parents work.

The first thing you have to do when your child doesn't feel well is determine what's wrong and whether or not to call the doctor. Then make your child comfortable, give her medicine if the doctor has prescribed it, and settle her down to rest, sleep, and drink lots of fluids.

If you work, you must have a backup plan in case of illness. Make arrangements beforehand, so you're not caught unprepared. A neighbor, relative, or a stay-at-home mom can help if your regular baby-sitter isn't available. Try to find a job where your employer understands that there may be days when you have to stay home with a sick child. Don't leave a sick child at home alone—you never know what might happen.

In cases of a more serious illness or hospital stay, put aside everything else in your life and give your child your undivided attention. Keep her fully informed about what's happening to her.

Many hospitals give guided tours to young patients, so the child knows where she'll be and has an idea of what's going to happen. Then it's much less scary. Take advantage of these programs— they're designed to alleviate a child's anxiety. Andrew had ear surgery twice last year, and the tours were reassuring for both him and his parents. Ask questions until you feel you've been fully informed, and don't let any health worker brush you off or intimidate you.

Be sure you don't reward sickness. When I was growing up, if we stayed home from school because we were ill, my mother's policy was to be appropriately sympathetic and to provide whatever care was indicated, but we had to stay in bed, rest, drink plenty of fluids, and eat bland, uninteresting foods. We were seldom sick, and never stayed sick for long—there wasn't much of a payoff in it.

98.

Teach Your Children About Sex

THERE ARE TWO DISTINCT areas relating to sexuality that you need to discuss with your children. The first is teaching them about their bodies. Simply stated, what it means to be a girl or a boy.

Talk to your kids about their anatomy, the changes one goes through on the road to adulthood, and what sorts of sexual feelings they may experience during their childhood and adolescence. They need to become intimately acquainted with their own bodies. Show them diagrams, and identify and discuss sexual organs.

The second area of discussion is about having a sexual relationship. Intercourse obviously plays an enormous part in this, but should be presented in terms of the whole picture: respect for one's partner, the responsibility for the relationship, the level of commitment it should involve, a deep understanding of the emotional side of a sexual relationship, and the necessity for preventing pregnancy and disease.

These are issues you cannot leave to your school or church to teach. Your values are not presented in a sex-education class. Your children probably have questions they're too embarrassed to ask in front of classmates, and you can't possibly know what more your children need to learn unless you have a frank discussion with them.

You may never have discussed sex with your own parents, and you may feel inhibited or embarrassed about discussing it with your children. But as more than one pediatrician I have talked to would say, get over it. You have to have these discussions. As they get older, a lack of information about pregnancy or AIDS can drastically affect your children's lives.

Here are some ideas for making these discussions easier:

Start their sex education when your children are very young. Make sure they know all the proper names for different parts of their bodies.

Watch sex education videos with them, beginning when they're five or six. There are numerous books and videos available for educating children of all ages about sex. Preview several to find ones with an approach you're comfortable with.

Be prepared. Read about and think about ways you'll respond when your children start to ask questions about their bodies or about where babies come from. Answer very honestly and simply, but don't give them more information than they've asked for. They'll let you know when they want to know more, especially if you've kept the lines of communication open by being forthcoming and natural with your answers. Again, books and sex education videos will help you here.

When interest in the opposite sex becomes evident, sit down for a heart-to-heart talk. Discuss respect, responsibility, feelings, and emotional consequences as well as pregnancy and sexually transmitted diseases. Discuss homosexuality. Make sure you've done all you can to insure your child's safety and happiness. Your teenagers also need to know about date rape, how to fend off unwelcome passes, and how to examine their own feelings and emotions.

Many parents worry that if they discuss sex and birth control with their kids, the kids will think the parents condone premature sexual behavior. But you can have a frank discussion and leave no doubt as to your position on the subject. And even more importantly, studies conducted by the Institute of Medicine at the National Academy of Sciences show that it's the kids who *don't* know the facts of life who get pregnant as teenagers or contract AIDS or other sexually transmitted diseases.

Also, when kids know about sex and appropriate sexual behavior, it gives them more control over their own bodies. It provides the understanding necessary to help them deter unwanted advances from peers as well as from adults.

Some parents assume that because their kids have seen so much sex on TV, or perhaps have talked with friends about sex, that they must know what it's all about. These are false and dangerous assumptions. And you can't impart your moral standards or answer their questions if you leave it to sexually explicit TV shows to inform your kids about sex.

The bottom line is that eventually your children will have sex— either before marriage or after—and when they do, they need to be fully informed. You won't be there to make their decisions for them, but what you've taught them may protect them from making huge, life-altering mistakes.

Remember that sex is normal and healthy, and it's our job as parents to help our children become mature, sexually responsible adults.

99.

Prohibit Cigarettes, Alcohol, and Drugs

STUDIES CONDUCTED by the National Center on Addiction and Substance Abuse at Columbia University show that children who do not smoke, drink, or do drugs between the ages of ten and twenty will probably never do so. The 1994 Surgeon General's report found that smoking cigarettes can lead to drug and alcohol abuse. Most marijuana users started by smoking cigarettes, and most serious drug abusers started by smoking pot. One form of substance abuse often leads to further abuse and experimentation with other substances.

So your best strategy is to make certain your teenagers do not start smoking, drinking, or doing drugs while in their teens. Here's how.

The most important step you can take to keep your kids off drugs is to make it absolutely clear to them that smoking, drinking, and drugs are not allowed—and never will be. Prohibit any of this behavior in your home. A casual attitude on your part sends the wrong message to your kids. The Columbia University report showed that kids whose parents firmly prohibit drugs are much less likely to experiment than kids whose parents don't forbid them.

Set a good example. If you don't smoke or drink yourself, your children are unlikely to begin. If you do drink, do so responsibly and in moderation, and never let your children see you drunk—or hear you say things like, "Boy, I sure need a drink."

When your children are between the ages of nine and eleven, start teaching them about the dangers of substance abuse. Repeat the lessons on a regular basis as they get older.

Avoid telling your kids directly that you don't like their friends. They'll stop talking to you about them. You'll then be cut off from information about who their friends are and the activities they're involved in.

Instead, get to know your kids' friends. Encourage them to come to your home. Talk to them, even though you think you may have nothing in common with someone with pink hair and a nose ring. Find a mutual interest beyond the appearances—music, sports, school, cars, movies, the weather. You'll get to know them for who they are, see how they interact, and learn which friends you can trust. And you'll be able to supervise your kids and their friends more closely.

Talk to the parents of your children's friends—agree on rules, curfews, and consequences. Let the kids know you're talking with one another. Vera regularly calls the parents of her kids' friends—

especially the parents she knows only casually—to confirm that their values are compatible with hers and Tim's. If she talks with parents who clearly don't have the same vigilance she does, she is much stricter about letting her kids accept party or overnight invitations.

Don't leave your children at home unsupervised, and make sure you're there when they have a party. Some kids crash parties where adults are not present. No matter how responsible your child is, other kids may take advantage of the situation.

When your child goes to a friend's house for a party, call to make sure that a parent is present and that alcohol is not being served. Amazingly, some parents actually provide beer or alcohol for their children's parties.

Teach your children to make responsible decisions regardless of the pressure they may feel from their peer group. Again, role-play actual situations they might encounter so they have the verbal tools to deal with these situations, and so they have a chance to think beforehand about how they'd react.

Get your child involved in sports, religious, or other after-school activities. Kids involved in extracurricular activities are less likely to smoke, drink, or do drugs.

Recognize signs of substance abuse. These include a change in academic performance; depression and withdrawal from the family; perhaps new, troublesome friends; a loss of interest in hobbies and activities; mood swings and other unexplainable changes in behavior that you know aren't normal for your child.

Never give up. Even if your child starts to experiment with smoking or you catch him drinking or doing drugs, stay on course. Be firm without nagging. Impose consequences like revoking car privileges—especially for drinking or doing drugs—moving up a curfew, or grounding him.

Get professional help. If you suspect that your child is drinking or using drugs on a regular basis, get help immediately. Call your physician or a drug hot line to find out what steps you should take to address the problem. Habits formed at this age are very difficult to break. Fix the problem before it ruins all of your lives.

Remove your child from the situation if you possibly can. Change schools, or send him to summer camp. Sign him up for any kind of Outward Bound–type program that will focus his attention on other things and give him the skills and the self-confidence to resist drugs and other temptations.

The sixteen-year-old son of a friend of mine got seriously involved with drugs. He went from being an honor student to failing his junior year in high school. Having tried everything else she could think of, my friend took him out of school for a year and sent him to work as a volunteer on a forest conservation crew. Within the year he had turned his life around. He is now completing his doctoral thesis in physics and has done outstanding work in his field.

Send your child to live with friends or relatives in another town, even for a short vacation, to give him a change of scenery, where he'll be less likely to be exposed to problems.

If you send your child to live elsewhere for a while, you'll still have to monitor him closely; you can't expect anyone else to parent with the same attention and devotion that you do. But if your child's well-being and future are in danger, do whatever you can to alter the situation.

Work on your child's self-esteem. A confident child who has the love and attention of his parents, is secure in his schoolwork, and is involved with outside activities has no reason to get high.

Fifteen

THE MOST
IMPORTANT THING

100.

Make a Date with Your Child

THE BUSINESS OF LIFE frequently takes up so much time that it's easy to get into the habit of giving our kids the time that's left over—if there is any. Our kids deserve better.

As we've seen, there are many things you can do to make life with your kids easier and more fun, and there's a lot you can do to free up more time to be with them. It'll improve the quality of your life a good deal when you can devote some time every day to each child—even if, to begin with, it's just a few minutes at bedtime.

Tim learned this when he started giving his kids ten minutes of undivided attention each evening when he got home from work, before the distractions of the evening set in. Their relationships to him changed dramatically when they stopped having to pester him to play, and they saw that he truly cared about them and their interests.

I've heard from many parents who've taken similar steps. One mother told me she started to make a concerted effort to spend more time with her previously out-of-control preschool daughters. She set up a play area in the living room. Now each evening when she comes home from work, she gives them her full attention for thirty minutes. She listens to stories about their day and allows them to decide what they want to do. They draw, paint, play house, and engage in any games or activities the kids decide on. Since she's been doing this her daughters have become much easier to manage, and the rivalry between the girls has greatly diminished.

Another couple I heard from has two sons, ages seven and eleven. From the time the boys were toddlers the parents have made a practice of each spending at least one hour one evening a week with each boy. On Mondays the mother spends time with the younger boy, the father spends time with the older one; on Thursday nights they switch kids. The parents have strong relationships with both boys, as the boys do with each other, and the parents feel this time together has contributed to the close ties they all share.

In addition to the time you spend with your kids in the normal course of your daily lives—the cooking, eating, driving, carpooling time—try spending one-on-one time with each child each week. Set aside less important obligations and activities, like shopping, talking on the phone, or mundane chores, and devote the time to your children. If you schedule the same time each week, and write it on your family calendar, it will increase the chances that you'll keep this date with your child and that you'll continue to keep it.

During this time give your child your undivided attention—turn off the TV, let the answering machine take your calls, and eliminate any other distractions. Don't preach, teach, lecture, or nag. Instead, talk to him about what he wants to talk about. Play the games he wants to play. Read the stories he wants to read.

A weekly date with each child will enhance the quality of your relationships, keep you in touch with the emotional and developmental stages of their lives, and give you an opportunity to enjoy and truly get to know each other. Your kids will be happier, better adjusted, and more willing to abide by the rules you set. And you'll be building close and loving relationships with your kids that will last a lifetime.

A Final Thought

THIS BOOK is meant to be used as a guide to help you negotiate many of the challenges parents face today. Your goal is to take the initiative and create a life that works for you. You want a family you enjoy, a job you like, a house you can manage, and enough money to pay the bills, with enough left over for vacations and retirement.

You can start by choosing just one idea from this book that will give you immediate relief. If you can relate to the harried parent at the beginning of the book who is overwhelmed by demanding kids, a sinkful of dirty dishes, and a phone that keeps on ringing, you could start by letting the answering machine pick up calls during the dinner hour. That one step could change the course of your entire evening.

If you're having a hard time getting your kids out of bed and off to school in the mornings, show them how to organize their clothes and books the night before. And get them to bed earlier.

If you're spending your afternoons and weekends as the family chauffeur, cut back on your kids' activities. And set up car-pool arrangements with other parents.

The next time your child starts to throw a tantrum, walk away. The drama ends when the audience leaves.

Try one thing at a time. Once you've integrated that into your routine, go on to another item that would help you simplify your life. Don't feel you have to use every technique I've mentioned. Some you may need; others might not work for you. And you'll come up with your own methods that will make your life with kids easier.

Be prepared for resistance—most children don't like change. And kids who are used to getting what they want by throwing a tantrum won't like it when you say no and mean it. But remember that your kids are looking to you for structure and firm guidance. They feel secure and well loved when you provide it, and their behavior will change as they get used to the new routine.

Simplifying is an ongoing process. By cutting back on the stuff, getting help with the household responsibilities, and fostering independence in your children, you can begin to arrange your day and your week so you're not always moving at a breathless pace—and you'll even find time for yourself. By creating relaxing mealtimes, enjoyable bath times, and snuggly bedtimes you can take advantage of the fleeting opportunities each day brings to get involved in your children's world and enjoy your kids for who they are.

When you maintain your patience and keep a sense of humor in dealing with the natural rivalries and disciplinary issues most families face, you'll have more confidence in your ability as a parent. As your parenting becomes more consistent and effective, you'll be rewarded with happy, well-adjusted children. And when you remember you *are* the parent, you can learn to enjoy the present and keep an eye on the future—and the mutual respect and lasting bonds wise parenting creates.

A Word of Thanks

I AM DEEPLY GRATEFUL to all the parents who took the time to read the manuscript and who so graciously shared the wisdom of their experience, most especially Tim Cole, Elaine and George Zavoico, Jane Dystel, Karin Kirk, Joanie Nicholas, Judie O'Brien, Carolie Noyes, Joni Andrews, Ellen Horsch, Catha Paquette, Joe Phillips, and my husband, Wolcott Gibbs, Jr. I am also grateful to all the readers, teachers, friends, and strangers who shared their ideas on simplifying.

My sincerest thanks go to Dr. Norman Weinberger for the time, energy, and expertise he contributed to the health chapter.

I want to thank everyone at Andrews McMeel Publishing. It has been a pleasure working with Tom Thornton, Chris Schillig, Jean Zevnik, JuJu Johnson, Esther Kolb, and all the other colleagues who greatly contributed to this book and who simplified my life in the process.

Most of all I am indebted to my dear friend Vera Cole for, among many other things, the patience, dedication, thought, hard work, late nights, early mornings, and generosity of spirit she put into this book. Without her this book would not have been written.

Dear Reader:

Because so many readers have asked for it, I am planning to put together a book of letters I've received from people who have simplified their lives. I've got long letters and short notes, funny stories and heart-warming sagas from people around the world who are starting or continuing to live more simply.

The book will include a chapter on simplifying with kids. If you have an interesting story about the process of simplifying your life or any tips on simplifying with kids that you'd like me to share with others through the book, you can write to me at the address shown below.

I may not be able to write back to everyone—I'm still trying to keep life simple—but I'd love to hear from you. Please be sure to let me know if I can include your name and town, or if you'd prefer to be identified only by your initials.

Elaine St. James
c/o Editorial Department
Andrews McMeel Publishing
4520 Main Street
Kansas City, MO 64111